Lincoln's Lover

Lincoln's Lover

Mary Lincoln

in

Poetry

SELECTED, ARRANGED, AND EDITED

BY

JASON EMERSON

The Kent State University Press

Kent, Ohio

© 2018 by The Kent State University Press, Kent, Ohio 44242
Poetry used by permission; for complete information, please refer to Acknowledgments.

Library of Congress Catalog card Number 2017038350
ISBN 978-1-60635-306-6
Manufactured in the United States of America

Library of Congress Cataloging-in-Publication Data
Names: Emerson, Jason, 1975- editor.
Title: Lincoln's lover : Mary Lincoln in poetry / selected, arranged, and edited by Jason
  Emerson.
Description: Kent, Ohio : The Kent State University Press, 2017. | Includes bibliographical
  references.
Identifiers: LCCN 2017038350 (print) | LCCN 2017055684 (ebook) | ISBN 9781631012921
  (epub) | ISBN 9781631012938 (ePDF) | ISBN 9781606353066 (pbk.)
Subjects: LCSH: Lincoln, Mary Todd, 1818-1882--Poetry. | Presidents' spouses--United
  States--Poetry. | Lincoln, Abraham, 1809-1865--Family.
Classification: LCC E457.25.L55 (ebook) | LCC E457.25.L55 L56 2017 (print) | DDC
  973.7092/2--dc23
LC record available at https://lccn.loc.gov/2017038350

Mary, the saddest name

In all the litanies of love

And all the books of fame.

—Patrick Kavanagh

Contents

CONTENTS   ix

Foreword

My husband grows hybridized daylilies in our backyard. Among these flowers are two with nearly identical blooms; and, as is often the case, the flowers have names of people, some related to the hybridizer, others named for people of importance or celebrity. The two flowers that look so much alike are named "Mary Todd" and "Norma Jean." Each is a large yellow blossom, among the most prominent in the garden, buxom and cheerful, the plants long-blooming and hardy. Until reading Jason Emerson's collection of poems by and about Mary Todd Lincoln, I thought "Norma Jean" fit this particular daylily, while "Mary Todd" did not. Why? Because I'd bought into the notion of Mary Todd as a troubled, materialistic, difficult woman, one more of a burden than helpmate to her long-suffering and tolerant husband Abraham.

Lincoln's Lover dispels that myth for me. Through these poems, a different portrait of the former First Lady emerges, one that presents a more complex picture, more humane, of a woman not only with flaws, but strengths, a woman who raised four children, often alone, busy as her husband was, a woman who suffered unspeakable tragedy and who loved her husband, and he her, with constancy and affection.

In "Riding on a Dray," Dr. E. H. Merriman presents a young Mary hitching an undignified ride in a common wagon to avoid walking home on muddy streets. This was obviously something young ladies of Mary's social class should know better than to do. "Up flew windows, out popped heads," Merriman writes, "To see this Lady gay / In a silken cloak and feathers white / A riding on a dray." To a twenty-first-century reader, this ballad projects Mary as quite modern, a woman who knows her own mind, is practical, strong-willed, unfazed by the inevitable gossip that will mark her as unrefined. Merriman, writing this poem in 1839/40, was not particularly impressed with Mary's behavior: "A moral I'll append / To this my humble lay / When you're sticking in the mud / Why call out for a dray."

There are poems in this collection, however, whose authors have great sympathy for Mary Lincoln. George Moses Horton, in "Mrs. Lincoln's Lamentation," presents Mary's grief over the death of her husband. In this 1865 poem she laments the absence of her husband as stealing her sense of herself as a woman. Her depression is depicted metaphorically in her perception of nature:

> Never more, never, hence to be a woman,
> Or thus bereft of all the nature dear!
> The lilies droop, the willows sadly weep,
> The garden is divested of her grace;
> For every scene is pendent as with grief,
> And desolation spreads the city around.

" . . . they do not dare / To see how lovely is the pain that marks / Your face, and drove the world about you to / The brink of nothing safe or sane or heard," writes Jason Emerson in his 2009 "Epistle to Mary Lincoln." Here the poet finds the grief of a nation over the devastation of the Civil War in the face of the president's wife, a mark of compassion for her husband's difficult responsibilities and decisions.

Rather than portraying the relationship of Mary and her husband as unloving and contemptuous due to her lavish spending, unpredictable temper, and erratic behavior, these poems provide evidence of Mary's devotion to Abraham and his reciprocal love and passion for her. A letter from Lincoln himself, its poetic prose written as lines, spells out his tenderness toward her:

In this troublesome world
we are never
quite satisfied. When you were here, I thought
you hindered me some
in attending to business;
but now, having nothing but
business—no variety—
it has grown
exceedingly tasteless to me.
I hate to sit down and direct documents,
and I hate to stay
in this old room
all by myself.

And Dan Guillory delves into the sexual attraction of Mary in his un-
sentimental depiction of her sensuality and desirability to her husband:

She of the endless purse—
Pillager of millinery shops,
Jewelry and cutlery
Copper silver gold
Brooches pearls pins
Necklaces bracelets gems
Flimsy tulle veils whalebone
Corsets and lacework shawls.

O, she of the burning gaze
The upcurled lip
The little finger
Hooked behind my ear
That hitching-post of love,

She of the marble knees
The alabaster throat
The breasts of cool pink jade
Nippled in coral.

("Litany for Mary T.")

The erotic nature of this 2007 poem is surely something one would expect more for the beautiful temptress "Norma Jean" than for the overweight, temperamental "Mary Todd." The imagery, however, reminds one of the "Song of Solomon," lifting its sensual imagery to a spiritual plane.

Were Mary Todd Lincoln traveling the roads in early summer in Lexington, Kentucky, she would have seen scores of the common orange, gangly daylilies that grow wild in ditches along the way. She would not know that one day a daylily would be named for her, representing the bright, headstrong, loving, sexy, misunderstood woman history has failed to share with us. The intriguing poems in *Lincoln's Lover* attempt to correct that misconception. I, for one, have been swayed.

Maureen Morehead
Kentucky Poet Laureate
March 31, 2012

Acknowledgments

First and foremost I offer my sincere thanks to all the poets and publishers who allowed me to reprint their works included in this book:

E. H. Merriman, "Riding on a Dray," originally published in "A Story of the Early Days in Springfield—And a Poem," *Journal of the Illinois State Historical Society* 16, nos. 1–2 (April–July 1923): 141–46.

Mary A. Denison, "To Mrs. Lincoln," and Emissus, "To Mrs. Lincoln," originally published in J. N. Plotts, ed., *Poetical Tributes to the Memory of Abraham Lincoln* (Philadelphia: J. B. Lippincott & Co., 1865), 81–83, 222–23.

George Moses Horton, "Mrs. Lincoln's Lamentation," originally published in George Moses Horton, *Naked Genius* (Raleigh, N.C.: Wm. B. Smith & Co., 1865), 155–57.

Sarah E. Carmichael, "President Lincoln's Funeral," originally published in Sarah E. Carmichael, *Poems* (Utah, 1866), 21–24.

Marion Mills Miller, "Lady of Lincoln," originally published in Thomas Del Vecchio, ed., *Contemporary American Male Poets: An Anthology of Verse by 459 Living Poets* (New York: Henry Harrison, 1937), 164.

Courtenay Fraser Fite, "The Spirit of Mary Todd Speaks," originally published in *Jackson* [Miss.] *Daily News,* Feb. 18, 1940.

Reed Miles Perkins, "Mary Todd Lincoln," originally published in Reed Miles Perkins, *Prairie Poems* (Springfield, Ill.: Frye Printing, 1946), 16.

Jane Merchant, "Valentine for Mary Lincoln," originally published in *Washington Star,* Feb. 14, 1955.

Della Crowder Miller, "Mary Visits Lexington: 1848–1849," and "Mrs. Lincoln Given Social Snubs: October 1861," originally published in Della Crowder Miller, *Abraham Lincoln: A Biographic Treatment in Sonnet Sequence,* 3 vols. (Boston: Christopher Publishing House, 1965), 2:82, 3:53.

Edward C. Lynskey, "Mrs. Lincoln Enters Bellevue Place," originally published in *College English* 49, no. 8 (Dec. 1987): 891.

Edward C. Lynskey, "Mrs. Lincoln's Epistle from Bellevue Place," originally published in *Commonweal* 124, no. 11 (June 6, 1997): 12.

Julianna Baggott, "Mary Todd on Her Deathbed," originally published in *Quarterly West* 48 (Spring/Summer 1999): 34–35; reprinted in *Best American Poetry 2000,* and in Baggott, *Lizzie Borden in Love: Poems in Women's Voices* (Crab Orchard Series in Poetry, 2006), 17–18.

Laurence Overmire, "Willie at the Foot of the Bed (An Ode to Mary Todd Lincoln)," originally published on Ancestry.com, 2003.

Kathleen Flenniken, "To Ease my Mind," originally published in *Iowa Review* 34, no. 2 (Fall 2004): 76; reprinted in Kathleen Flenniken, *Famous* (Univ. of Nebraska Press, 2006): 69–70, by permission of the University of Nebraska Press. Copyright © 2006 by the Board of Regents of the University of Nebraska.

Dan Guillory, "'Love Is Eternal'—November 4, 1842," and "Litany for Mary T.," originally published in Dan Guillory, *The Lincoln Poems* (Mahomet, Ill.: Mayhaven Publishing, 2007), 48–49, 52–55.

Julianna Baggott, "An Open Letter to Mrs. Lincoln," originally published on Quickmuse.com, October 2008.

R. T. Smith, "Mary Lincoln Triptych," originally published in the Winter 2012 issue of *The Missouri Review.*

I also am indebted to the Board of Trustees of the Mary Todd Lincoln House in Lexington, Kentucky, for allowing me to use a copy of their previously unpublished Mary Lincoln portrait, painted by Lloyd Ostendorf, as an illustration; and to the Batavia Depot Museum in Batavia, Illinois, for the use of their portrait of Bellevue Place Sanitarium.

Special thanks to James Cornelius, curator of the Abraham Lincoln Presidential Library and Museum, not only for the wonderful afterword he contributed to this book, but also for helping find a few of these obscure poems for me.

Introduction

Poets once were the constellations of their age, shining brightly, untouched, above the common mass of people, showing us all the path to our better natures and ambitions. Poetry was once the universal baptism for all great events: births and deaths, weddings and funerals, public speeches, gatherings, and dedications. The words of the poets rang forth and generations still read and listen. Why? The great eighteenth-century Romantic poet William Wordsworth said a poet was someone who said ordinary things in an extraordinary way. Irish poet Seamus Heaney said at the end of the twentieth century that poetry is not only "a matter of proffered argument and edifying content but . . . a matter of angelic potential, a motion of the soul."[1] Perhaps this is the allure of poetry: it offers everyone an inspirational way to perceive the world.

In fact, poetry and history have a long, intimate connection. Much of what we know about ancient history throughout the world came to us through the centuries and millennia as epic poetry purporting to tell the stories of great men and events. Some of the best-known examples include Homer's *Iliad* and *Odyssey*, Virgil's *Aeneid*, Ovid's *Metamorphoses*, the Portuguese *Lusiads*, the German *Nibelungenlied*, the Spanish *El Cantar de mio Cid*,

---

1. Seamus Heaney, *The Redress of Poetry* (New York: Farrar, Straus and Giroux, 1995), 192.

Beowulf, and the Irish legend of Cu Chulainn. Aristotle, in his *Poetics,* said a historian and a poet do not differ from each other because one writes in verse and the other in prose—"But they differ in this, that the one speaks of things which have happened, and the other of such as might have happened. Hence, poetry is more philosophic, and more deserving of attention, than history." While many would disagree that poetry is more deserving of attention than history, it is easy to see that history and poetry create a fascinating juxtaposition when viewing each through the lens of the other. To consider the life of a historical person through poetry—as in the present book—is to both see that person for who they were, and to consider who that person could have, or even should have, been in a more poetically perfect world.

Poets, as such, are often the harbingers of apotheosis. They recognize and celebrate greatness often before such greatness is realized by the larger population. As Ralph Waldo Emerson declared, "The sign and credentials of the poet are, that he announces that which no man foretold. . . . He is a beholder of ideas, and an utterer of the necessary and casual."[2] Some of the great poems in world history are elegy, such as John Milton's "Lycidas," Percy Shelley's "Adonais," and Alfred Tennyson's "The Lady of Shalott." One of Abraham Lincoln's favorite poems was Thomas Gray's "Elegy Written in a Country Churchyard." America's greatest elegy—some might argue its greatest poem—is Walt Whitman's "When Lilacs Last in the Dooryard Bloom'd," a somber tribute to Abraham Lincoln in the wake of the president's assassination.

Lincoln and poetry, in fact, have a long and intimate connection. As a young man, Lincoln wrote and even published multiple poems, and all of his greatest writings and speeches—especially the Gettysburg Address and Second Inaugural—are themselves outstandingly and inherently poetic. The poetry that Lincoln read and loved throughout his life, and its influence on him, forms a major part of every biographical study of him. There was even a 2008 book, *Lincoln: The Biography of a Writer,* which examined Lincoln from this literary angle.[3]

---

2. Ralph Waldo Emerson, "The Poet," in Emerson, *Essays* (Boston: Houghton, Mifflin and Company, 1890), 15.

3. Fred Kaplan, *Lincoln: The Biography of a Writer* (New York: HarperCollins, 2008).

Immediately after Lincoln's death, hundreds of poetic tributes to the martyred president were published in newspapers across the country. A number of these poems were collected and published that same year as *Poetical Tributes to the Memory of Abraham Lincoln*. Since then, the art of portraying or praising Lincoln in verse has never abated. Multiple book collections of poetry about Lincoln have been published, such as *The Praise of Lincoln: An Anthology* (1911), *The Poets' Lincoln: Tributes in Verse to the Martyred President* (1915), *The Book of Lincoln* (1919), and *Lincoln and the Poets* (1965).

Some of the greatest poems about Lincoln have been written by America's greatest poets: Herman Melville, William Cullen Bryant, John Greenleaf Whittier, James Russell Lowell, Stephen Vincent Benét, and, of course, Walt Whitman. Lincoln has been the literary muse for countless writers and poets of all skill levels, and continues to be so to this day.

But what about his wife, Mary?

Some might argue that Mary Lincoln is insufficient as muse or even as historical subject. And while she did not alter the course of American history as did her husband, she certainly contributed to his achievements. Mary Lincoln deserves attention not only as Abraham's wife, but also and especially as an astonishing woman and person in her own right. Mary Lincoln, similar to her husband, also has a long and intimate connection to poetry. In fact, this shared connection was one of the mutual interests that drew Mary and Abraham together as a couple when they first met.

As a young girl, Mary Todd, the daughter of a wealthy and influential banker and politician in Lexington, Kentucky, showed a predilection and passion for poetry. She had twelve years of formal schooling—more than nearly all women at the time, as well as most men—and was well read in classic literature. She found great pleasure and solace in verse. Her cousin remembered that as a young girl, Mary's "love for poetry, which she was forever reciting, was the cause of many a jest among her friends. Page after page of classic poetry she could recite and liked nothing better."[4] The bookshelves of the Todd home where Mary grew up were well stocked with

4. Mary Bradley Rally, "Cousin and Childhood Friend of Mary Todd Lincoln Tells of Days When She and Martyr's Wife Were Girls Together," *Lexington Herald*, Feb. 14, 1909, 1.

volumes of poetry by Robert Burns, Lord Byron, William Shakespeare, Alexander Pope, and other classics.[5]

Mary and Abraham often would read, recite, and discuss poetry together, both during their courtship and after their marriage. Mary was an earnest and voracious reader, and liked to "review" many of the volumes for her husband. "I heard him say he had no need to read a book after Mary gave him a synopsis," recalled Mary's younger sister Emilie Todd Helm.[6] Some of the known books of poetry owned by the Lincolns in Springfield included the works of Robert Burns, Eliza Cook, Oliver Goldsmith, Fitz-Greene Halleck, A. C. Reed, and William Shakespeare, as well as an anthology of female American poets edited by T. B. Read and a collection of "elegant extracts" of poetry compiled by Rev. Vicesimus Knox. Mary Lincoln also was a subscriber to the *Southern Literary Messenger,* a literary periodical.[7]

Mary, like her husband, loved the poems of William Shakespeare and Robert Burns, and instilled her love of poetry in her children, often reading to them from her favorite poets.[8] Her sister Emilie remembered Mary reading Walter Scott's poetry to her eleven-year-old son, Robert, who imbibed it so well that one day Mary and Emilie heard "sounds of strife" outside the Lincoln home and ran to the window to investigate. They saw Robert and a friend "having a battle royal," enacting scenes of Scott's poem,

5. Sale at Auction of Household and Kitchen Furniture of Robert S. Todd Estate, Lexington, Ky., Sept. 26, 1849, copy from Mary Todd Lincoln Home, Lexington, Ky.; William H. Townsend, *Lincoln and His Wife's Home Town* (Indianapolis: Bobbs-Merrill, 1929), 156–59.

6. Katherine Helm, *True Story of Mary, Wife of Lincoln* (New York: Harper & Brothers, 1928), 108.

7. Katherine B. Menz, *Lincoln Home Historic Furnishings Report* (Harper's Ferry, W.V.: National Park Service, 1984): Historical Data, Section D, available online at: http://www .nps.gov/history/history/online_books/liho/sectiond.htm. Letters between Mary and her oldest son Robert in 1876 mention her owning volumes of poetry by John Greenleaf Whittier, Alexander Pope, Elizabeth Barrett Browning, and Edward Bulwer-Lytton. Robert Lincoln to Mary Lincoln, Chicago, Feb. 7, 1876, Robert Todd Lincoln Letterpress Books, vol. 1, reel 1, pp. 162–64, Abraham Lincoln Presidential Library, Springfield, Ill.; Mary Lincoln to Robert Lincoln, Springfield, June 19, 1876, Justin and Linda Levitt Turner, *Mary Todd Lincoln: Her Life and Letters* (New York: Alfred A. Knopf, 1972), 615–16.

8. In 1869, Mary and Tad traveled throughout Scotland, during which they visited the home of Robert Burns. Mary described the visit in letters by telling of the sights they saw that Burns had immortalized in his poems. Mary Lincoln to Eliza Slataper, Frankfurt, Aug. 21, 1869, and to Rhoda White, Cronberg, Aug. 30, 1869, Turner and Turner, *Mary Todd Lincoln,* 512, 516.

"The Lady of the Lake," Emilie recalled. "Bob, with his sturdy little legs wide apart, was wielding a fence paling in lieu of a lance and proclaiming in a loud voice, 'This rock shall fly from its firm base as soon as I.' Mary, bubbling with laughter, called out, 'Grammercy, brave knights. Pray be more merciful than you are brawny.'"[9]

William Herndon, Abraham Lincoln's law partner, recalled that it was Mary's custom during a party "to dress up and trot out" her children "and get them to monkey around, talk, dance, speak, quote poetry, etc."[10] While to Herndon such antics were ridiculous, to Mary, raising children who were well dressed, intelligent, and literary was a mark of culture. Mary's teachings influenced oldest son Robert, who enjoyed reading poetry his entire life.[11] But it was middle son Willie who seems to have inherited his parents' facility with words. He even published an original poem in the Washington *National Republican* newspaper in 1861, when he was only ten years old, after the death of his father's close friend, Col. Edward D. Baker.[12]

9. Helm, *True Story of Mary*, 108. An 1847 copy of Scott's book *Lady of the Lake*, inscribed by Mary Lincoln to her cousin Helen M. Morse—and perhaps even the very same book Mary read to Robert—is part of the Lincoln archival collection (call number PR 5308.A1 1847), at the Abraham Lincoln Library and Museum, Harrogate, Tenn. In April 1858, Robert Lincoln borrowed volume 2 of Walter Scott's *Poetical Works* from the Illinois State Library. Amy Louise Sutton, "Lincoln and Son Borrow Books," *Illinois Libraries* 48, no. 6 (June 1966): 444.

10. William Herndon to Jesse Weik, Jan. 8, 1886, Emanuel Hertz, *The Hidden Lincoln: From the Letters and Papers of William H. Herndon* (New York: Viking Press, 1938), 128.

11. Robert Lincoln's home, Hildene, still has dozens of books of poetry on its shelves. Some of the poets Robert and his family enjoyed reading include famous writers such as Burns, Whittier, Longfellow, Tennyson, Browning, Milton, and Byron, as well as lesser-known poets like Isaac Rusling Pennypacker, Felicia Hemans, John A. Joyce, Thomas Campbell, William Newell, Wallace Bruce, and Mark Akenside. List of books provided by Brian Knight, former curator, Hildene, the Lincoln Family Home, Manchester, Vt.

12. Baker, colonel of the 71st Pennsylvania Infantry and a sitting U.S. senator from Oregon, was killed at the Battle of Ball's Bluff in Oct. 1861. The poem was published in the Washington *National Republican*, Nov. 4, 1861, page 1:

There was no patriot like Baker,
    So noble and so true;
He fell as a soldier on the field
    His face to the sky of blue.

His voice is silent in the hall,
    Which oft his presence grac'd,
No more he'll hear the loud acclaim,
    Which rang from place to place.

In 1860, an Eastern friend of the Lincolns' oldest son Robert visited the Lincolns in Springfield and was delighted to find that Mary Lincoln was "a lover of poetry." He gave her a copy of a book of poems by his friend Albert Laighton, selections of which she asked him to read aloud to her. She then brought the book with her to Washington in 1861.[13]

As first lady, Mary was allowed a $250 government appropriation to purchase books for the White House library. Being a lover of literature she reveled in the opportunity. In July and August of 1862, Mary spent the money on dozens of books, including volumes of poetry by Thomas Hood, Oliver Goldsmith, Elizabeth Barrett Browning, Lydia Huntley Sigourney, Frances Sargent Osgood, Edmund Spenser, and William Shakespeare.[14]

Mary kept her literary penchant vibrant by meeting and discussing literature and poetry with Massachusetts senator Charles Sumner, a true aristocrat and intellectual, and also a friend of Whittier, Longfellow, Emerson, and other New England writers. Mary herself befriended famous poets, such as N. P. Willis, editor of the *Home Journal* magazine, who formed part of her White House coterie. Willis was a vain man, according to Mary's cousin Elizabeth Grimsley, and one day he suddenly asked Mrs. Lincoln "You do not approve of me, you think me a very wicked man, say, truly, do you not?" Mrs. Lincoln asked in return "how could that be with one who wrote such exquisite sacred poems, that have been made ours,

---

No squeamish notions filled his breast,
    The *Union was* his theme,
'No *surrender and no compromise,*'
    His day thought and night's dream.

His country has her *part* to play,
    To'rds those he left behind,
His widow and his children all,
    She must always keep in mind.

13. Frank Fuller, *A Day with the Lincoln Family* (New York: Hotel Irving, 1905), 2; Albert Laighton, *Poems* (Boston: Brown, Taggard, and Chase, 1859).

14. Mary Lincoln to Benjamin Brown French, July 26, 1862, in Turner and Turner, *Mary Todd Lincoln,* 129–30; "Book purchases for the Library of the Executive Mansion," in Harry Pratt, *Personal Finances of Abraham Lincoln* (Springfield, Ill.: Abraham Lincoln Association, 1943), 180–81.

even through our school readers, where we and our children have learned to love them?"[15] As historian Ruth Painter Randall quipped, "Poetry was always an open sesame to Mary."[16]

The following collection contains poetry written by, for, and about Mary Lincoln. It is arranged chronologically by poem rather than by topic to avoid creating a muddled amalgamation of poetic styles from different centuries that would undoubtedly leave an erratic and uneasy impression on the reader. The collection begins with a rhymed and metered poem written in 1839 about an incident involving a young Mary Todd, and ends with a modern series of poems written in 2012 that give voice to Mary's infamous shopping, belief in spiritualism, and arrest on charges of insanity.

The chronological order not only arranges the poetic style of the works, but also offers a view of the changing perceptions of Mary Lincoln through the years. The first four poems show Mary as a living person contending with everyday issues. The four poems honoring Mary immediately after her husband's murder offer a glimpse of the public sympathy for the bereaved widow. The twentieth- and twenty-first-century poems show Mary as she is popularly seen today: as insane woman, as complex person, and as an intricate and indispensable part of her husband, Abraham Lincoln.

Interestingly, poetry written about Mary both during her life and in death has been sympathetic, seeking to understand and commiserate with a woman who reached a pinnacle of personal and political achievement only to be surrounded and overwhelmed by personal tragedy. This is surprising considering that Mary Lincoln is the most controversial first lady in American history, and her reputation has often been more negative than positive. Her biography shows that her gracious and generous nature, her keen intelligence, her love and support of her husband, all were—and remain—overshadowed by her quick temper, her jealousy and paranoia, and her illicit behaviors as first lady.[17]

15. Elizabeth Todd Grimsley, "Six Months in the White House," *Journal of the Illinois State Historical Society* 19 (Oct.–Jan. 1926–27): 68–69.

16. Ruth Painter Randall, *Mary Lincoln: Biography of a Marriage* (Boston: Little, Brown and Company, 1953), 240.

17. For examinations of Mary's negative qualities, which are generally glossed over in typical biographies of her, see Michael Burlingame, "The Lincolns' Marriage: 'A Fountain of

It is believed by many historians—yet disputed by others—that Mary suffered some form of mental and/or emotional illness, most likely bipolar disorder, which ultimately led her son Robert to commit her to an insane asylum in 1875.[18] This remains Mary's most conspicuous legacy, and a number of the poems about her focus on this aspect of her life. Yet there is more to the verses about her printed here, as there was more to Mary herself, than that one lamentable moment. There are verses concerning her relationship with her husband, such as their physical passion and emotional love for each other. There are sympathetic paeans to Mary as tragic widow of a murdered husband. There also are various reflections on Mary as young girl, as mother, and as first lady. Finally, there are elegies to Mary that wring out not only her own trials, but also her place in history and in her husband's great apotheosis.

So why do we, or why should we, care about Mary Lincoln or her connection to poetry? As Emerson said, "the experience of each new age requires a new confession." The study of Mary Lincoln as woman, wife, and widow currently is undergoing a renaissance. There have been at least twenty-four books (nonfiction, fiction, and juvenile) and four major stage productions on Mary Lincoln's life published since the turn of the twenty-first century, with more on the way. Her life and importance have only begun to be delved into. To experience her words, thoughts, and legacy as explained and exposed through poetry over the past one hundred seventy years advances our understanding and appreciation of this iconic individual.

Of course, there is another reason to read a book of poetry about Mary Lincoln. For enjoyment. The poet Dylan Thomas once told an admirer,

---

Misery, of a Quality Absolutely Infernal'" in *The Inner World of Abraham Lincoln* (Urbana: University of Illinois Press, 1994), 268–355; and Burlingame, "Mary Todd Lincoln's Unethical Conduct as First Lady" in *At Lincoln's Side: John Hay's Civil War Correspondence and Selected Writings* (Carbondale: Southern Illinois University Press, 2000), 185–203.

18. James S. Brust, "A Psychiatrist Looks at Mary Lincoln," in *The Mary Lincoln Enigma* (Carbondale: Southern Illinois University Press, 2012), 237–58; Jason Emerson, *The Madness of Mary Lincoln* (Carbondale: Southern Illinois University Press, 2007); Mark E. Neely and R. Gerald McMurtry, *The Insanity File: The Case of Mary Todd Lincoln* (Carbondale: Southern Illinois University Press, 1986).

"Read the poems you like reading. Don't bother whether they're 'important,' or if they'll live. What does it matter what poetry *is* after all? If you want a definition of poetry, say: 'poetry is what makes me laugh or cry or yawn, what makes my toenails twinkle, what makes me want to do this or that or nothing,' and let it go at that. All that matters about poetry is the enjoyment of it, however tragic it may be. All that matters is the vast undercurrent of human grief, folly, pretension, exaltation, or ignorance, however unlofty the intention of the poem."[19]

Thomas's words capture exactly the reason a collection such as this book has value. It is not only pleasant and interesting to read the verses about Mary Lincoln written over the years, but in Mary's life we find personified the full gamut of human emotion and experience.

19. Dylan Thomas, "Poetic Manifesto," in Thomas, *Early Prose Writings,* Walford Davies, ed. (London: J. M. Dent & Sons, 1971), 160.

1839–1840

Twenty-year-old Mary Todd left her father's house in Lexington, Kentucky, in the fall of 1839 for an extended visit with her sister, Elizabeth (Mrs. Ninian W.) Edwards in Springfield, Illinois. Mary quickly became friends with a young neighbor, Miss Mercy Levering, of Baltimore, who was visiting her brother. At some point during that winter of 1839–1840, constant rains turned the unpaved streets in Springfield to mud, leaving the girls housebound for three weeks. Finally, Mary—always vibrant and energetic—had had enough and invited her friend to go with her downtown. Mary had a bundle of shingles that she planned to drop in the mud and hop across until they made their way to the sidewalks on Monroe Street.

Either the shingles ran out or the girls got tired of their adventure, because Mary hailed Ellis Hart, driver of a two-wheeled wagon called a dray, and asked for a ride back to the Edwards House. Drays were used for hauling goods, not people, and Mercy refused to ride in it, afraid of the scandal such an uncouth sight would cause regarding the two well-bred, well-dressed girls. Young Mary insouciantly left her friend mired in the mud and rode alone, causing quite a sensation in the upper social circles of Springfield. One young man, Dr. E. H. Merriman, who moved in those same circles, saw the spectacle and composed a poem, which was circulated around the town.

Mercy Levering secured a copy and kept it the rest of her life. In 1923, her daughter gave a copy to the Illinois State Historical Society, which published it later that same year in its society journal.[1]

Riding on a Dray

As I walked out Monday last
A wet and muddy day
'Twas there I saw a pretty lass
A riding on a dray, a riding on a dray.
Quoth I sweet lass, what do you there
Said she good lack a day
I had no coach to take me home
So I'm riding on a dray.
At Lowry's house I got aboard
Next door to Mr. Hay
By yellow Poll's and Spottswood then
    A riding on a dray.
The ragged boys threw up their caps
And poor folks ran away
As by James Lamb's and o'er the bridge
    I plodded on my way.
Up flew windows, out popped heads,
To see this Lady gay
In a silken cloak and feathers white
    A riding on a dray.
At length arrived at Edwards' gate
Hart back the usual way.
And taking out the iron pin
    He rolled her off the dray.

---

1. "A Story of the Early Days in Springfield—And a Poem," *Journal of the Illinois State Historical Society* 16, nos. 1–2 (April–July 1923): 141–46.

When safely landed on her feet
Said she what is to pay
Quoth Hart I cannot charge you aught
   For riding on my dray.
An honor such as this
I meet not every day
For surely I'm the happiest man
   That ever drove a dray.
A moral I'll append
To this my humble lay
When you are sticking in the mud
   Why call out for a dray.

Dr. E. H. Merriman

1842

The only poem that Mary Lincoln ever admitted writing (though probably not the only one she did write, considering her love of poesy) was published in the Springfield, Illinois, *Sangamo Journal* in 1842, part of a piece of political satire that nearly caused her future husband to fight a duel.

In August and September 1842, a series of four satirical letters by "Rebecca," an uneducated but shrewd backwoods woman from "Lost Townships," appeared in the *Journal* ridiculing Democrat State Auditor James Shields for his political maneuvers concerning bank and tax issues. Whig State Assemblyman Abraham Lincoln, age thirty-three, wrote at least one of the "Rebecca" letters—the second one—published on September 2, 1842.[1] After he showed his letter to his paramour Mary Todd, age twenty-four, and her friend Julia Jayne, the girls contributed their own piece to the series, the fourth letter, which was published on September 8. While the previous "Rebecca" letters had ridiculed Shields's politics, the Todd/Jane letter debauched him personally. Their contribution, among other things, ridiculed him for being offended at the previous letters and for seeking "satisfaction" from the anonymous author. The final installment of the "Rebecca" correspondence in the *Sangamo Journal* was a poem published on September 16, 1842, and signed "Cathleen." It celebrated the "marriage"

---

1. Abraham Lincoln, "The Rebecca Letter," Aug. 27, 1842, Roy P. Basler, ed., *Collected Works of Abraham Lincoln* (New Brunswick, N.J.: Rutgers University Press, 1953), 1:291–97. For an examination of the letters and the subsequent events, see Roy P. Basler, "The Authorship of the 'Rebecca' Letters," *Abraham Lincoln Quarterly* 2, no. 2 (June 1942): 80–90.

between Shields and the rough-hewn Rebecca who was "not over sixty, and am just four feet three in my bare feet, and not much more round in girth"; and lamented all the hearts left broken by the nuptial of the vain and pompous Shields.[2]

Shields was so incensed by the final two "Lost Townships" items that he accosted the newspaper editor and demanded to know the identity of the author. Lincoln chivalrously took responsibility. Shields immediately insisted a public retraction, and when Lincoln refused, Shields challenged him to a duel. Lincoln accepted and, as the challenged party, chose the weapons—broadswords. He later said he did not want to hurt his opponent, but if forced to would have split him from head to toe. Lincoln probably would have achieved this easily given his great advantage of reach, Shields being seven inches shorter in stature. Because dueling was outlawed in Illinois, the men and their seconds traveled to a spot in Missouri across the Mississippi River from Alton, Illinois. At the last minute, friends of both men convinced each to retract their offensive statements, shake hands, and return to Springfield.[3]

The famous Shields duel incident humiliated Lincoln, and he and Mary agreed never to discuss it. In February 1865, an army officer heard the tale and asked President Lincoln if the story of the duel, "all for the sake of the lady by your side," was true. Lincoln, flushed by embarrassment replied, "I do not deny it, but if you desire my friendship, you will never mention it again."[4]

In December 1865, Mary wrote about the duel in three separate pieces of correspondence in six days, and in each letter she claimed authorship of the "Cathleen" poem. She explained to one friend, "Gen. Shields, a kindhearted, impulsive Irishman, was always creating a sensation and mirth, by his drolleries. On one occasion, he amused me exceedingly, so much so, that I committed his *follies,* to rhyme, and very silly verses they

2. Untitled poem, *Sangamo Journal,* Sept. 16, 1842.

3. For the series of correspondence concerning the duel, see Abraham Lincoln to James Shields, Sept. 17, 1842, and "Memorandum of Duel Instructions to Elias H. Merryman," Sept. 19, 1842, and "Statements Concerning the Whiteside-Merryman Affair," Oct. 4, 1842, Basler, *Collected Works,* 1:299–302.

4. Mary Lincoln to Francis B. Carpenter, Dec. 8, 1865, Turner and Turner, *Mary Todd Lincoln,* 298–99.

were, only, they were said to abound in sarcasm causing them to be very offensive to the Genl. A gentleman friend, carried them off and persevered in not returning them, when one day, I saw them, strangely enough, in the daily paper."[5]

⚓

Ye jews-harps awake! The ——'s won—
Rebecca the widow has gained Erin's son;
The pride of the north from the Emerald isle
Has been woo'd and won by a woman's sweet smile.
The combat's relinquished, old loves all forgot:
To the widow he's bound, Oh! bright be his lot!
In the smiles of the conquest so lately achieved.
Joyful be his bride, "widow's modesty" relieved,
The footsteps of time tread lightly on flowers—
May the cares of this world ne'er darken their hours.
But the pleasures of life are fickle and coy
As the smiles of a maiden sent off to destroy.
Happy groom! in sadness far distant from thee
The Fair girls dream only of past times of glee
Enjoyed in thy presence; whilst the *soft blarnied store*
Will be fondly remembered as relics of yore,
And hands that in rapture you oft would have prest,
In prayer will be clasp'd that your lot may be blest.

Cathleen

5. Emphasis in original. Mary Lincoln to Mary Jane Welles, Chicago, Dec. 6, 1865, ibid., 295–96. See also Mary Lincoln to Josiah G. Holland, Chicago, Dec. 4, 1865, ibid., 292–93.

1848

Few letters between Abraham and Mary Lincoln are known to exist. One reason is that while preparing for their move to the White House in 1861, Mary, in a typical nineteenth-century action of "breaking up house-keeping," burned a number of personal letters and papers in the backyard. A neighbor stopped the destruction and took home some of the letters.[1] It also is known that the oldest Lincoln son, Robert, burned a number of family papers that he considered "purely private" and inappropriate for public reading.[2] Specifically, Mary wrote in the mid-1860s about having a box in which she kept the personal letters of her husband, which she would take out and read periodically.[3] These letters never have been found, and are exactly the type of materials Robert would have destroyed to protect his parents' privacy.

The majority of surviving pieces of correspondence between husband and wife are brief telegrams during the White House years. However, two wonderful pieces from 1848 do exist, and have become the most well-known

1. Carl Sandburg, *The Lincoln Collector: The Story of the Oliver R. Barrett Lincoln Collection* (New York: Bonanza Books, 1960), 71–72.

2. James T. Hickey, "Robert Todd Lincoln and the 'Purely Private' Letters of the Lincoln Family," in *The Collected Writings of James T. Hickey* (Springfield: Illinois State Historical Society, 1990), 159–79; Jason Emerson, *Giant in the Shadows: The Life of Robert T. Lincoln* (Carbondale: Southern Illinois University Press, 2012), 403–4.

3. "This morning I have been looking over and arranging a large package of his dear, loving letters to me, many of them written to me, in the 'long ago,' and quite yellow with age." Mary Lincoln to Mary Jane Welles, near Chicago, July 11, 1865, Turner and Turner, *Mary Todd Lincoln*, 257.

and often-quoted letters concerning the marriage. They were written while Lincoln, then a member of the U.S. House of Representatives, was in Washington and Mary, four-year-old Robert, and two-year-old Eddie, were staying at the Todd home in Lexington.

They are sweet, chatty letters about simple family items: Lincoln buying socks for Eddie, asking how the boys liked the letters he sent them, and even flirting with Mary by asking about her weight; Mary wrote about her aunt and uncle, her stepmother ridding the house of a cat Eddie wanted to keep and his subsequent screams, and of making clothing for the boys. But they also show the love and passion between husband and wife, stated in words of longing to be together rather than apart.[4]

Abraham Lincoln was certainly a poet. He wrote poems, published at least one in the newspaper, and, as is universally agreed, his later writings and speeches as politician and president today are considered great prose poems.[5] Respected poet, historian, and academic Marion Mills Miller (who has his own poem on Mary Lincoln in this volume), even stated that had Lincoln chosen literature over politics as his life's work, he would have written some of the best poetry ever produced in America. As an example of Lincoln's inherent poetic nature, Miller poeticized the Gettysburg Address.[6] Likewise, Fred Kaplan, in his recent book, *Lincoln: The Biography of a Writer,* poeticized part of an 1859 Lincoln speech on agriculture.[7]

Lincoln's famous love letter to his wife, dated April 16, 1848, was not versified by him, but, when rearranged typographically, it is poetic. It

4. Abraham Lincoln to Mary Lincoln, Washington, Apr. 16, 1848, Basler, *Collected Works,* I:465–66. Mary's response also exists: Mary Lincoln to Abraham Lincoln, Lexington, May—, 1848, Turner and Turner, *Mary Todd Lincoln,* 36–38.

5. Abraham Lincoln, *The Poems of Abraham Lincoln,* Little Books of Wisdom Series (Bedford, Mass.: Applewood Books, 1991); James Raymond Perry, "The Poetry of Lincoln," *North American Review* (Feb. 1911): 213; R. Gerald McMurtry, "Abraham Lincoln: Poet," *Lincoln Lore* 529 (May 29, 1939) and "Lincoln: Poet or Rhymester?" *Lincoln Lore* 1484 (Oct. 1961); Jason Emerson, "The Poetic Lincoln," *Lincoln Herald* 101, no. 1 (Spring 1999): 4-12; Richard Lawrence Miller, "Lincoln's 'Suicide' Poem: Has It Been Found?" *For the People: A Newsletter of the Abraham Lincoln Association,* 6:1 (Spring 2004): 1, 6.

6. Marion Mills Miller, "The Poetic Spirit of Lincoln," in Osborn H. Oldroyd, ed., *The Poets' Lincoln* (Washington, D.C., 1915), v.

7. Fred Kaplan, *Lincoln: The Biography of a Writer* (New York: HarperCollins, 2008), 303.

becomes a free-verse poem filled with alliteration, assonance, and consonance, along with a liltingly anapestic rhythm punctuated with two iambic moments that slow the movement and enhance the emotion.

Dear Mary

From a letter by Abraham Lincoln,
April 16, 1848

In this troublesome world
we are never
quite satisfied.
When you were here, I thought
you hindered me some
in attending to business;
but now, having nothing but
business—no variety—
it has grown exceedingly
tasteless to me.
I hate to sit down and direct documents,
and I hate to stay
in this old room
all by myself.

Abraham Lincoln

1850

Historians are certain of only one poem written by Mary Lincoln, the anonymous poem signed "Cathleen" from 1842. But for more than half a century, historians debated about a second poem that she could have written—and some writers even declared unflinchingly that she did compose.

The first great tragedy in the Lincoln family—in what would become a terrible tradition of family tragedies—was the death of Abraham and Mary's second child, Edward. Three-year-old "Eddie," as the family called him, was always a sickly child. In December 1849, he became seriously ill with consumption—or pulmonary tuberculosis—for which there was no known cure. For fifty-two days and nights Abraham and Mary worriedly nursed their son while Eddie lingered; but on February 1, just weeks short of his fourth birthday, the boy died.[1]

Mary, only thirty-one years old at the time, was so distraught by the loss that she shut herself in her room for days and refused to eat or sleep, forcing her husband finally to plead, "Mary, you must eat, for we must live."[2] Abraham suffered profoundly, but his only written mention of his loss, simple and painfully controlled, came three weeks later when he informed his stepbrother, "We lost our little boy . . . . We miss him very much."[3] On

1. U.S. Census 1850, Mortality Schedule for Springfield, Sangamon Co., Ill., 787, MS., Illinois State Archives; Untitled announcement, *Illinois Daily Journal*, Feb. 2, 1850.
2. Mrs. John Todd Stuart, interview with *Chicago Tribune*, Feb. 12, 1900, John G. Nicolay Papers, LOC; Octavia Roberts, *Lincoln in Illinois* (Boston: Houghton Mifflin, 1918), 67.
3. Abraham Lincoln to John D. Johnston, Feb. 23, 1850, Basler, *Collected Works of Abraham Lincoln*, 1:76.

February 2, after a funeral service in the Lincolns' home, Eddie was laid to rest in Hutchinson's Cemetery. Five days later, an unsigned poem titled, "Little Eddie," was published in the *Illinois Daily Journal* newspaper.[4]

Since 1954, Lincoln scholars have speculated and debated over whether Mary or Abraham wrote the poem, mainly because the last line, "of such is the kingdom of Heaven," was engraved on Eddie's tombstone. But exactly which of the dead boy's parents wrote the verse was a mystery. Both Mary and Abraham read and wrote poetry, although none of their existing creations resembles Eddie's poem in diction or structure, and no mention of the poem has ever been found in any of their letters.[5]

In 1954, historian Harry Pratt suggested it was Abraham who wrote the poem, while in 1987 writer Jean H. Baker unabashedly asserted that "Little Eddie" was "a mother's production" due to its feminine language and maternal endearments.[6] The main arguments in favor of Abraham's authorship are that he seems to have written more poetry than his wife, and, most importantly, he could handle the loss and pain of death, while Mary could not. Debilitating and inconsolable grief were Mary's trademarks after every family tragedy. Could she muster the strength and presence of mind to compose such a moving poem? Or was the act of writing a catharsis for her overwhelming grief?

The answer to the mystery was revealed in 2012, when historian Samuel P. Wheeler discovered that Mary Lincoln did not write the poem; rather, it was penned by a St. Louis woman in 1849 "who most likely had no knowledge of the Lincoln family."[7] Since "Little Eddie" was published in the *Illinois Daily Journal* "by request," the poem was most likely published in a St. Louis newspaper and seen by either Abraham Lincoln or someone close to the Lincoln family and reprinted in honor of Eddie Lincoln.

4. "Little Eddie," *Illinois Daily Journal*, Feb. 7, 1850.

5. For a full examination of the poem and its possible authorship, see Jason Emerson, "'Of Such Is the Kingdom of Heaven': The Mystery of Little Eddie," *Journal of the Illinois State Historical Society* 92, no. 3 (Autumn 1999): 201–21.

6. Harry Pratt, "Little Eddie Lincoln–We Miss Him Very Much," *Journal of the Illinois State Historical Society* 47, no. 3 (Autumn 1954): 300; Jean H. Baker, *Mary Todd Lincoln: A Biography* (New York: W. W. Norton & Co., 1987), 126.

7. Samuel P. Wheeler, "Solving a Lincoln Literary Mystery: 'Little Eddie,'" *Journal of the Abraham Lincoln Association* 33, no. 2 (Summer 2012): 34–46.

Even though "Little Eddie" has been proven not to be a Mary Lincoln composition, the poem's history and the decades of disagreement over its authorship have made it a fascinating story within Lincoln lore, and have earned it a place in the Mary Lincoln poetry canon.

Little Eddie

Those midnight stars are sadly dimmed,
  That late so brilliantly shown,
And the crimson tinge from cheek and lip,
  With the heart's warm life has flown—
    The angel of Death was hovering nigh,
    And the lovely boy was called to die.

The silken waves of his glossy hair
  Lie still over his marble brow,
And the pallid lip and pearly cheek
  The presence of Death avow.
    Pure little bud in kindness given,
    In mercy taken to bloom in heaven.

Happier far is the angel child
  With the harp and the crown of gold,
Who warbles now at the savior's feet
  The glories to us untold.
    Eddie, sweet blossom of heavenly love,
    Dwells in the spirit-world above.

Angel boy—fare thee well, farewell
　Sweet Eddie, we bid thee adieu!
Affection's wail cannot reach thee now,
　Deep though it be, and true.
　　Bright is the home to him now given,
　　For, "of such is the kingdom of Heaven."

Anonymous

1862

During her lifetime, Mary Lincoln had many admirers, just as she had legions of detractors. Similarly, while nearly all the poetry inspired by Mary Lincoln is laudatory, there are some pieces that are not at all complimentary. Such is the case of "The Queen Must Dance," published anonymously in the February 9, 1862, issue of the Philadelphia *Sunday Dispatch* newspaper. The poem is a stinging satire of Mary Lincoln's decision to hold an invitation-only presidential ball while the country was in the midst of a Civil War and soldiers were suffering on the battlefields and in the field hospitals.

The ball, which was held on February 5, 1862—only seven months after the Union disaster at First Manassas and less than four months after the Union rout at Ball's Bluff—saw more than five hundred of the capital's elite citizens spend the night at the White House reveling in exclusivity and consuming huge amounts of food and drink, all purchased with government money. The dinner was considered "one of the finest displays of gastronomic art ever seen in this country. It was prepared by Maillard of New York, and cost thousands of dollars," reported the *Boston Daily Advertiser.* "The tables fairly bent under expensive luxuries heaped one upon another."[1]

As was the journalistic custom of the time, newspapers explained in detail the fashions of all the ladies present, especially Mrs. Lincoln. It was reported that the first lady wore a white satin dress with a train a yard in

1. "Mrs. Lincoln's Ball," *Boston Daily Advertiser,* Feb. 7, 1862, 2.

February 1862 presidential gala hosted by President and Mrs. Lincoln. Originally printed in *Leslie's Illustrated Weekly,* Feb. 22, 1862. Courtesy Library of Congress Prints and Photographs Division, Washington, D.C.

length, trimmed with black lace flounces festooned up with white and black ribbon. "The dress was, of course, décolleté and with short sleeves displaying the exquisitely molded shoulders and arms of our fair 'Republican Queen,' the whiteness of which were absolutely dazzling," reported *Frank Leslie's Illustrated Newspaper.* "Her head-dress was a coronet wreath of black and white crape myrtle, which was in perfect keeping with her regal style of beauty." Her jewelry consisted of pearl necklace, earrings, brooch, and bracelets.[2]

2. "The Presidential Party," *Frank Leslie's Illustrated Newspaper,* Feb. 22, 1862, 214. See also "The Ball at the White House," *Springfield* [Mass.] *Republican,* Feb. 8, 1862, 5; "The Entertainment at the White House Last Night," [Washington, D.C.] *Evening Star,* Feb. 6, 1862, 2.

George H. Boker. Courtesy Library of Congress Prints and Photographs Division, Washington, D.C.

Presidential secretary John Nicolay wrote to his fiancée the day after the ball that it was "a brilliant success," while Ben: Perley Poore, a journalist and Washington insider, later wrote of the evening that "it was compared to the ball given by the Duchess of Richmond at Brussels the night before Waterloo."[3] Yet, despite the ball's success—or maybe because of it—the criticism of the Lincolns, and Mary in particular, was merciless. The *New York Herald* called the event "A social blunder greatly to be regretted"; the *Sandusky* [Ohio] *Register* called the event "so out of all sympathy with the travail of the Nation, that no plea can excuse it"; while the *Cleveland Herald* said it was "about as appropriate as a game feast and gallopades at a funeral" and compared it to "a burning Rome and a fiddling Nero."[4]

What all of these critics did not apparently know or understand was that the Lincolns attended their ball that evening with hearts full of anxiety over their eleven-year-old son Willie, who was sick in bed on the second floor of the Executive Mansion. Willie had been ill for some days, most likely with typhoid fever, and the Lincolns nearly canceled the ball until their doctor said Willie was improving. Still, the president and first lady left their guests multiple times during the party to go upstairs and sit with their sick boy. Two weeks later, Willie died.

This was the climate in which George H. Boker, a prominent Philadelphia poet and playwright, penned "The Queen Must Dance." According to Boker's biographer, the poet's satire "merely expressed a disapprobation which was general. It was severe, but it was sincerely meant and widely recopied."[5]

3. John G. Nicolay to Therena Bates, Feb. 6, 1862, John G. Nicolay Papers, Library of Congress. Ben: Perley Poore, *Reminiscences of Sixty Years in the National Metropolis*, 2 vols. (Philadelphia: Hubbard Brothers Publishers, 1868), 2:120.

4. "The Ball at the White House," *Springfield* [Mass.] *Republican*, Feb. 8, 1862, 5; "The Ball at the White House," *Sandusky Register*, Feb. 12, 1862, 2; "The Ball at the White House," *Cincinnati Daily Press*, Feb. 8, 1862, 2.

5. Edward Sculley Bradley, *George Henry Boker: Poet and Patriot* (Philadelphia: University of Pennsylvania Press, 1927), 202–3. This poem was not, however, ever printed in any of Boker's later collections of poetry.

This and following page: Handwritten manuscript of George Boker's 1862 poem "The Queen Must Dance," a scathing satire of First Lady Mary Lincoln's decision to hold an invitation-only grand fete in the midst of the Civil War. Courtesy George H. Boker papers (Ms Coll. 661), Kislak Center for Special Collections, Rare Books and Manuscripts, University of Pennsylvania.

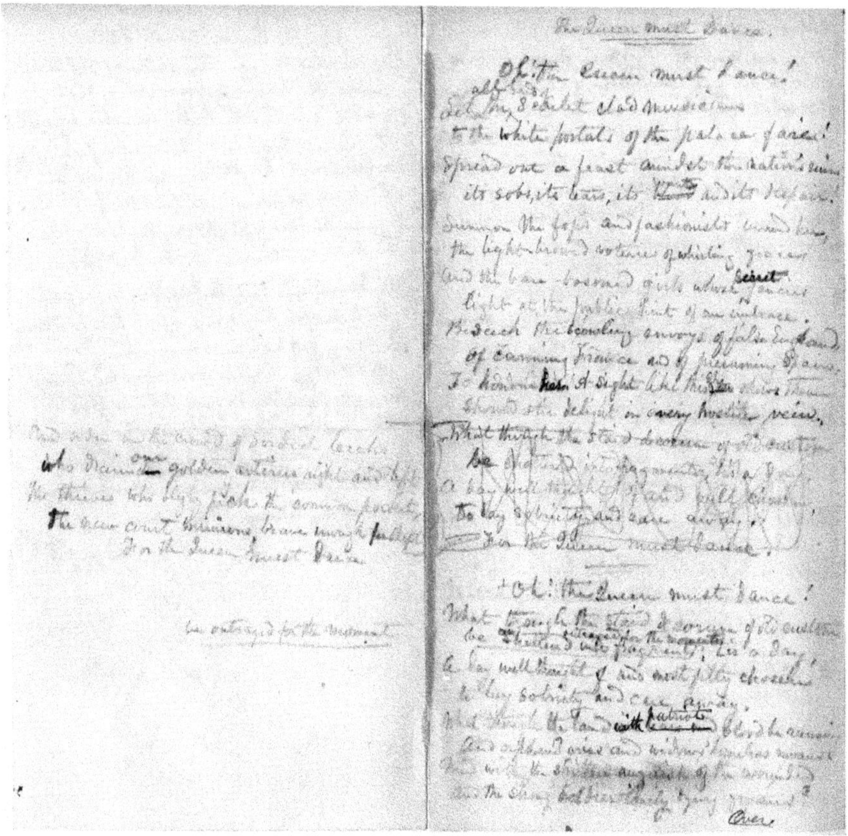

The Queen Must Dance

Oh! The Queen must dance!
Set all the band of scarlet clad musicians
    to the white portals of the palace fare!
Spread out a feast amidst the nation's ruins,
    its sobs, its tears, its wants and its despair!
Summon the fops and fashionists around her,
    the light-browed votaries of whirling grace,
And the bare-bosomed girls whose secret fancies
    light at the public hint of our embrace.
Beseech the scowling envoys of false England,
    of cunning France and of presuming Spain,
To honor her. A sight like this she shows them
    should stir delight in every hostile vein.
And order in the crowd of sordid leeches
    who drain our golden arteries right and left,
The thieves who slyly pick the common pocket,
    The new court eminence, brave enough for theft
    For the Queen must dance.

Oh! The Queen must dance!
What though the staid decorum of old custom
    be outraged for the moment; tis a day,
A day well thought of and most fully chosen
    to lay sobriety and care away.
What though the land with patriot blood be running
    and orphaned cries and widows' homeless moans
Mix with the shrilled anguish of the wounded
    and the strong soldier's lonely dying groans?
What though the sick man through his narrow window,
    can see the light and hear joyous strains,

And on his loathsome pillow gasps distracted
    at what may appears seem an insult to his pains?
I charge you, maids and matrons of Columbia,
    to veil your faces and this thing disown.
Let her disport herself amongst her fiddlers
    alone, yes, in God's awful sight, alone!
    If the Queen must dance!

    Oh the Queen must dance!
Ah! woman, woman, doff your gaudy velvets,
    your foreign laces and your flashy rings
And clothe your vanity in decent raincoat
    and busy you about more holy things.
Go to the sufferer like the English Florence,
    call back his life or ease his dying grief,
Let all his pressing wants find ministering
    from you whence justly he may claim relief.
And let us see you flitting by the camp-fire,
    take the rough soldier by his honest hand,
Lift his overlabored hopes with charming spirits,
    and he shall bless your name throughout the land,
Were it not better, than half leagued with traitors,
    and quite suspected, to enact a part
That glitters to the vulgar fancy only
    and shows no traces of either brain or heart,
    If the Queen must dance?

    Oh! The Queen must dance!
Like Hebrew Miriam, then, strike up the timbrel
    before the heroes of your native West;
The first who used the empty gun and bayonet,
    the foremost soldiers of the war confessed.

Nor yet forget the patient ranks awaiting
   the tardy winter, for the land they love;
There is no hand uplifted in this struggle
   that is not consecrate by God above.
Oh! Dance and sing before these noble soldiers
   and make their courage equal their great cause,
A cause on which the nation's future glory
   rests as great nature rests upon her laws.
On with the strong banner to the outposts!
   Where'er it waved of right in days of yore;
And close behind it, treading on to music,
   Let the thick columns of our warriors pour;
   If the Queen must dance.

George H. Boker

1865

The assassination of President Abraham Lincoln at Ford's Theatre on Friday, April 14, 1865, was a seminal moment not only for the country, but especially for Mary Lincoln. That afternoon, she and her husband had taken a carriage ride around the city of Washington and discussed their plans for life after the presidency. After years of toil and emotional burden, the president finally was relieved, and both Lincolns felt a rekindling of their relationship that had been strained by years of war. "During the drive he was so gay that I said to him, laughingly, 'Dear Husband, you almost startle me by your great cheerfulness,' he replied, 'and well I may feel so, Mary, I consider *this* day, the war, has come to a close," Mary later wrote.[1]

At Ford's Theatre that night, watching a performance of *Our American Cousin* in the company of young Clara Harris and her fiancé Major Henry R. Rathbone, Mary was supremely happy, and smiled and leaned against her husband several times. "What will Miss Harris think of my hanging on to you so?" she whispered contentedly to her husband. "She won't think anything of it," the president replied. When assassin John Wilkes Booth fired the fatal shot into Lincoln's brain during act 3, scene 2, Mary Lincoln was holding her husband's hand.[2]

1. Emphasis in original. Mary Lincoln to Francis Bicknell Carpenter, Nov. 15, 1865, Turner and Turner, *Mary Todd Lincoln*, 284–85. See also Mary Lincoln to Mary Jane Welles, July 11, 1865, ibid, 257.

2. Helen (Bratt) DuBarry to "My dear Mother," Washington, D.C., Apr. 16, 1865, SC 425, Manuscripts Division, Abraham Lincoln Presidential Library, Springfield, Ill.; Dr. Anson G. Henry to his wife, Apr. 19, 1865, Lincoln Miscellaneous Manuscripts, Folder 8, Box 4, Department of Special Collections, University of Chicago Library; Mary Lincoln to Edward Lewis Baker Jr., Apr. 11, 1877, in Turner and Turner, *Mary Todd Lincoln*, 633.

Mary Lincoln spent the five weeks after the assassination confined to her White House bedroom, refusing all callers except the closest family and friends. She later characterized that time as "a bed of illness and many days and nights of almost positive derangement."[3] The entire country pitied and sympathized with the president's widow, and newspapers across the country printed updates on her health and misery for weeks after the assassination.[4]

The assassination caused an outpouring of national grief unlike anything in American history up to that time. Politicians clamored to eulogize the first martyred president, clergymen gave thoughtful sermons upon Lincoln's life and achievements on that Easter Sunday, and artists of all varieties used their works to honor the dead. The great deluge of verbal mourning and veneration was led by America's poets.

In the nearly one hundred fifty years since Lincoln's death, numerous poems and collections of poetic paeans to "Father Abraham" have been published. The first such compilation, *Poetical Tributes to the Memory of Abraham Lincoln,* printed mere months after the president's assassination, contained tributes not only to Abraham Lincoln, but also two "To Mrs. Lincoln" offering comfort and commiseration for the widow.[5] The first of these two poems was signed with the pen name "Emissus" and datelined Charleston, South Carolina. The second was written by Mary Andrews Denison, a prolific nineteenth-century writer. Denison wrote more than eighty novels throughout her life, and contributed stories, poems, and juvenilia to numerous popular periodicals, including *Frank Leslie's Monthly, Harper's Weekly,* the *People's Home Journal,* and *Youth's Companion.* During the last two years of the Civil War, her husband was a hospital chaplain in Washington, D.C., and Mary served as a volunteer nurse.[6]

---

3. Mary Lincoln to Mrs. Kasson, Chicago, Jan. 20, 1866, Lincoln Collection, Abraham Lincoln Presidential Library, Springfield, Ill.

4. For example, see "News From Washington," *New York Times,* May 1 and 12, 1865, 1.

5. J. N. Plotts, ed., *Poetical Tributes to the Memory of Abraham Lincoln* (Philadelphia: J. B. Lippincott & Co., 1865), 81–83, 222–23.

6. Margaret Sullivan Burke, "The Home of Mrs. Mary A. Denison," *The Writer* 7, no. 1 (Jan. 1894): 3–4; Mary E. Ireland, "Mary A. Denison," *Magazine of Poetry* 7, no. 2 (Feb. 1895): 108; *Boston Evening Transcript,* Oct. 17, 1911.

To Mrs. Lincoln

Oh! Gracious God, do lend thine ear,
    In tender love and zeal,
To this heart-rending, humble prayer,
    And this sincere appeal,
For her whose heart is bow'd in grief,
    For him she loved so dear—
Who finds nor comfort nor relief,
    Tho' constant tears appear.

Lord, give her strength to cast aside,
    This mournful wail of mind,
With trusting heart let her confide,
    That she may surely find
Comfort from those who love her true,
    With constancy replete,
From faithful breasts where friendship grew
    And blooms so pure and sweet.

Severe affliction has been thrown
    Upon her earthly peace;
While sorrow's web has quickly grown
    To bind without release:
Her life's upon a stormy sea,
    Tossed by a gloomy gale,
Along the shores where troubles flee
    Deep in a dolesome vale.

Father, her mind with rapture lift
    To Christian's brightest scope
Of heavenly joy—this precious gift
    Will give her strength to hope

That all her trials shall allay
   Into a peaceful form
Of happiness, to drive away
   Affliction's darkest storm.

And tho' her heart be fully clothed
   With Mary's sinful grief,
More sinful yet, may be betrothed
   With murmuring for relief,
Yet give her strength to purge the sin
   By pure and contrite heart,
Till truly cleansed, without, within,
   And all her sins depart.

The floating clouds around, portray
   Such dark and dismal hues:
Oh! Lord, disperse this sad array,
   Into refreshing dews,
To spread the path with righteous grace,
   With holy light of love;
Which sacred gift let her embrace,
   'Twill all her grief remove.

The cares entrusted to her guide,
   Her dearest comfort be;
Whose years, I pray, may gently glide
   In peace o'er life's sad sea.
While blooming in capacious mind
   In wisdom's fertile grove,
May gather thence the wisest kind
   Of knowledge from above.

Then let the brightest pleasures roll
   Across her peaceful breast,
Until the solemn knell shall toll
   Her breath to silent rest.
Then may her soul but realize
   The blessing from above,
Eternal joys—the only prize
   Of God's redeeming love.

As twilight hours doth softly link
   Day's beauties with the night;
And as the morning beams shall drink
   The darkness from the light:
So may death as gently fling
   His mantle o'er her eyes,
While angels, with protecting wings,
   Shall waft her to the skies.

Emissus

1865

To Mrs. Lincoln

If it be any joy to know
That a whole nation mourns thy woe;
That clasped hands and bowed down head
Bear witness for the mighty dead;
That he was loved as ne'er before
A chief in peace or chief in war;
Take this one drop of balm—and less
By that thy draught of bitterness!

If it be any joy to feel
That thine is now the national's weal;
That every home would gladly be
A shelter, and a shrine for thee;
That every heart throbs high to make
Some sacrifice for his own dear sake:
Take this one thought of comfort,—less
May be thy draught of bitterness.

If it be any joy to see
One glimpse of thy high destiny,
As she who wore a martyr's love—
And wears an angel's now, above—
As she who felt the throbs that swelled
That heart, by hearts of millions knelled:
Take this sweet sympathy—and less
By that thy draught of bitterness!

Oh! wife of our dear patriot—see—
Our land sheds tear for tear with thee;
Yet, widow of the nation! God
Speaks to thee, through the broken sod;
"I am thy God—thou yet shall see
It was not death, but victory!
And even now my love shall bless
And drain thy cup of bitterness."

Mary A. Denison

1865

Of all the poets who versified over Mary Lincoln (and Abraham Lincoln) in the wake of the assassination, perhaps the most unique was former slave George Moses Horton, the "Black Bard of North Carolina."

Horton was a slave for sixty-eight years, from his birth in 1797 until the close of the Civil War. Unable to write, Horton composed poems in his head and recited them aloud before receiving the help of a white woman (possibly Caroline Lee Hentz, a poet and novelist) who wrote his poetry down and helped him publish his first book.[1] He learned to write at age thirty-one. For years thereafter, still a slave but allowed by his master to spend his time and earn money writing, Horton wrote and sold multiple poems a week to various journals and newspapers across the country, as well as to college students in Chapel Hill, North Carolina.

His first two volumes of verse, *The Hope of Liberty* (1829) and *The Poetical Works of George Moses Horton, The Colored Bard of North Carolina* (1845), were published while he was still in bondage. When Union troops entered Chapel Hill in 1865, Horton came under their protection. He traveled with the soldiers to the North, writing poems about the war's end. His final collection, *Naked Genius*, was published in 1865. It contained a poem titled, "Lincoln Is Dead," honoring the martyred President Lincoln—an exceptional poem not included in any anthology of verse about Lincoln's

1. Stephen B. Weeks, "George Moses Horton: Slave Poet," *The Southern Workman* 43, no. 10 (October 1914): 572.

death—and also a verse titled "Mrs. Lincoln's Lamentation," lamenting the death of the president and sympathizing with his widow's loss.[2]

Horton's biographer, Joan R. Sherman, writes of the bard, "His achievements as a man and a poet were extraordinary: Horton was the first American slave to protest his bondage in verse; the first African American to publish a book in the South; the only slave to earn a significant income by selling his poems; the only poet of any race to produce a book of poems *before* he could write; and the only slave to publish two volumes of poetry while in bondage and another shortly after emancipation."[3]

Horton died in Philadelphia at age eighty-six.

Mrs. Lincoln's Lamentation

What is it for the breezes seem to wail,
The sylvan warblers carol nature's sighs,
For lo! he dies, but leaves behind his name
Eternal Lincoln! weep ye pensive bards,
Loud orators declaim with rills of tears,
For sorrow must attend the dol'rous scene!
Ye damsels of the city weep, O Washington,
Whence is our father fled, gone, gone forever!
Father Abraham the sample of faith,
Whence goest though to—.
Try the wonders of eternal worlds, but
Still we mourn, but we could not go with thee,
The lady of thy love aspires to thee.
Weep! O my soul, my quick pulse beat thy last,
Ye portals of immortal worlds fly wide,
Eternal messenger go tell my spouse,

2. George Moses Horton, *Naked Genius* (Raleigh, N.C.: Wm. B. Smith & Co., 1865), 155–57.
3. Joan R. Sherman, *The Black Bard of North Carolina: George Moses Horton and His Poetry* (Chapel Hill: University of North Carolina Press, 1997), i.

To meet me at the threshold of the city,
For lo! I come in haste from nature's gloom,
Seraphic groups descend and waft me home!
O, Abraham, descend at once and open wide thy bosom,
Ye bright attendant bands escort me hence,
Let me look down on the sulphrous gulf,
And view the rich man with his blistered tongue,
The damned, the infernal homicide of peace,
While loud he calls and beckons for relief!
O, father Abraham, send down one drop
Of cooling water to appease the wound,
But ah! too late, the fratrid murderer cries,
My friend, my father Abram, bears me home;
I'm on my way, I'm on my way to heaven.
But oh! the scene is closed and leaves me drear,
Imagination's dream has passed away,
And I awake again, alas! to weep!
Surviving friends, my Abram is no more,
No more to see me till I pass away;
O strike the fatal primogenial blow,
Let me into chaos and oblivion
Never more, never, hence to be a woman,
Or thus bereft of all the nature dear!
The lilies droop, the willows sadly weep,
The garden is divested of her grace;
For every scene is pendent as with grief,
And desolation spreads the city around.
The theatre's gloomy where he fell,
With doors and windows closed, where is then
The brave, the glorious, and the friend of man?
The grave is his asylum, death his friend,
At which from gloom the country rose to light,
On war's last eve the sun of glory sets,

The disk is called in gloom, the star of peace
Break forth in his expanse reflecting glory,
O'er a benighted hemisphere, he leaves
The blaze of day thrown back on every eye.

George Moses Horton

1866

Of all the poems published about Abraham Lincoln's death in 1865, one of the most popular was "President Lincoln's Funeral" by Utah poet Sarah E. Carmichael. Carmichael was a Mormon living in Salt Lake City, but her objection to polygamy and her marriage to an army doctor of non-Mormon background somewhat alienated her from the local community.

Carmichael's first signed poem, "Truth," appeared in the *Deseret News* in 1858 when she was twenty years old. The poem was so well crafted that some people doubted its authorship. Hundreds of her poems were published in local and national newspapers during the next eight years, and Carmichael often was called a literary genius. She received national recognition when revered poets William Cullen Bryant and May Wentworth anthologized her poems.[1]

Carmichael's only book of verse, *Poems,* was published in 1866 by a group of her friends and admirers. That same year she married army surgeon Jonathan M. Williamson, who had been stationed at Camp Douglas. Shortly after her marriage, Carmichael suffered a mental breakdown of unknown origin and stopped writing poetry. She was widowed in 1882, and spent her last years in a mental hospital. She died childless in 1901.[2]

---

1. May Wentworth included Williamson's poems "A Christmas Rhyme" and "Sorrow" in her collection, *Poetry of the Pacific: Selections and Original Poems from the Poets of the Pacific States* (Pacific Publishing Company, 1867); and William Cullen Bryant anthologized "The Stolen Sunbeam," retitling it "The Origin of Gold" in *The Family Library of Poetry and Song* (New York: Fords, Howard, and Hulbert, 1870).

2. Susan Howe and Sheree Maxwell Bench, eds., *Discoveries: Two Centuries of Poems by Mormon Women* (Salt Lake City: Brigham Young University, 2004), 95.

Toll! Toll!
All mortal life is brief.
Toll! Toll!
Toll! Toll!
Weep for the nation's chief!

Bands of mourning draped the homestead,
And the sacred house of prayer;
Mourning folds lay black and heavy
On true bosoms everywhere:
Yet there were no tear-drops streaming
From the deep and solemn eye
Of the hour that mutely waited
Till the funeral train went by.
Oh! there is a woe that crushes
All expression with its weight!
There is pain that numbs and hushes
Feeling's sense, it is so great.

Strongest arms were closely folded,
Most impassioned lips at rest;
Scarcely seemed a heaving motion
In the nation's wounded breast;
Tears were frozen in their sources,
Blushes burned themselves away;
Language bled through broken heart-threads,
Lips had nothing left to say.
Yet there was a marble sorrow
In each still face, chiseled deep;
Something more than words could utter,
Something more than tears could weep.

Selfishly the nation mourned him,
Mourned its chieftain and its friend;
Eye no traitor mist could darken,
Arm no traitor power could bend;
Heart that gathered the true pulses
Of the land's indignant veins,
And, with their tempestuous spurning,
Broke the slave's tear-rusted chains:
Heart that tied its iron fibers
Round the Union's starry band;
Martyr's heart, that upward beating,
Broke on hate's assassin hand!
Oh! the land he loved will miss him,
Miss him in its hour of need!
Mourns the nation for the nation
Till its tear-drops inward bleed.

There is one whose life will mourn him,
With a deep, unselfish woe;
One who owned him chief and master
Ere the nation named him so.
That the land he loved will miss him
Does she either think or care?
No! the chieftain's heart is shrouded,
And her woman's world was there:
No! the nation was her rival;
Let its glory shine or dim,
He hath perished on its altar—
What were many such to him?

Toll! Toll!
Toll! Toll!
Never again—no more—
Comes back to earth the life that goes
Hence to the Eden shore!

Let him rest!—it is not often
That his soul hath known repose;
Let him rest!—they rest but seldom
Whose successes challenge foes.
He was weary—worn with watching;
His life-crown of power hath pressed
Oft on temples sadly aching—
He was weary, let him rest.

Toll, bells at the Capital!
Bells of the land, toll!
Sob out your grief with brazen lungs—
Toll! toll! toll!

Sarah E. Carmichael

Abraham Lincoln's Funeral on Pennsylvania Avenue, Washington, April 19, 1865.
Brady-Handy Photograph Collection, Library of Congress Prints and Photo-
graphs Division, Washington, D.C.

1937

Perhaps the most poignant poem about Mary Lincoln ever published was written at the turn of the twentieth century by Dr. Marion Mills Miller. Miller, a scholar of classical literature at Princeton University, wrote poetry and fiction, but was best known for his work in translation and history. He compiled, edited, or translated numerous multivolume works on Greek and Latin literature and American history throughout his life, but one of his passions was the life and legacy of Abraham Lincoln.

Miller edited a nine-volume "centenary" edition of *The Life and Works of Abraham Lincoln* in 1907 in anticipation of the centennial celebration of Lincoln's birth. In 1908, Miller edited a small book of extracts from Lincoln's speeches and writings called *The Wisdom of Lincoln* and in the same year edited a previously unpublished manuscript called the *Life of Lincoln* by Henry Clay Whitney. Whitney was one of Lincoln's friends and legal colleagues who had earlier written the book, *Life on the Circuit with Lincoln.* Although Whitney is credited as the author of his two-volume *Life* and Miller as the editor, the second volume, *Lincoln, the President,* was mostly written by Miller. In 1915, Miller aided Osborn H. Oldroyd with the latter's collection of poetic tributes to the sixteenth president, *The Poets' Lincoln.* Miller assisted with the editing of the book, wrote an essay on "The Poetic Spirit of Lincoln" as the introduction, and composed an original poem on "Lincoln and Stanton" for inclusion.

Miller's only known poetic effort concerning Abraham Lincoln's wife, "Lady of Lincoln," was anthologized in 1937; its original publication has proven impossible to locate.[1] Mary Lincoln's niece Katherine Helm quoted the concluding stanza of Miller's poem on the title page of her 1928 family-authorized biography, *True Story of Mary, Wife of Lincoln*. It is unknown if Robert Lincoln or his wife Mary Harlan Lincoln, both of whom encouraged and assisted Helm with her book, contributed to the decision to use the quotation—although it is possible.[2] Charles Stoltz also used the quote in the introduction to his 1931 booklet, *The Tragic Career of Mary Todd Lincoln*.

Miller's poem was written at a time when Mary Lincoln's legacy and reputation was a matter of much disagreement. Books and articles discussing Mary either considered her an exceptional woman and wife, or reviled her as a relentless termagant constantly nagging and burdening her husband. "Lady of Lincoln," is the first known poem about Mary Lincoln that sought to understand who she was, how she contributed to her husband's success, and how her memory had been maligned.

✧

Lady of Lincoln

Lady of Lincoln,
　Little bride
Whose love uplifted
　His fallen pride.

Lady of Lincoln,
　Loyal mate
Whose faith in his greatness
　Made him great.

---

1. Thomas Del Vecchio, ed., *Contemporary American Male Poets: An Anthology of Verse by 459 Living Poets* (New York: Henry Harrison, 1937), 164.

2. A search of the bookshelves at Hildene, Robert Lincoln's home in Manchester, Vt., which contains his family's book collection largely intact, did not uncover any of Miller's works.

Lady of Lincoln,
   Patriot soul
Whose love of country
   Embraced the whole.

Lady of Lincoln,
   They wreathed her head
With thorns when living,
   With nettles though dead.

Marion Mills Miller

1938

When considering Mary Lincoln's historical role as wife and lover of Abraham Lincoln, it also has become necessary—whether rightly or not—to consider and compare her to Ann Rutledge, Lincoln's first love when he was a young man in the pioneer village of New Salem, Illinois. Such a comparison and contrasting is especially essential in the realm of poetry, thanks to a 1915 poem by Edgar Lee Masters that has become an American poetical classic.

New Salem was a small village of less than a dozen houses and 100 inhabitants in the wilds of Illinois when twenty-two-year-old Abraham Lincoln landed there in 1831. It was there he became a shopkeeper, postmaster, surveyor, politician, and, ultimately, began his study of the law as a profession. It was also there he met Ann Rutledge, daughter of the local tavern keeper.

Ann, it was later said, was pretty, slender, friendly, and compassionate. "She had as gentle and kind a heart as an angel, full of love, kindness, sympathy. She was beloved by everybody and everybody respected and loved her, so sweet and angelic was she," one New Salem resident said. Abraham and Ann fell in love and became engaged, but before they could marry she contracted "brain fever" and died. Lincoln was devastated; his friends later said he was "deranged" with grief and supposedly could not stand the thought of rain and snow beating on her grave; when speaking of Ann's death and grave he reportedly said, "My heart lies buried there."[1]

1. W. G. Greene, interview by William Herndon, Douglas L. Wilson, and Rodney O. Davis, eds., *Herndon's Informants: Letters, Interviews, and Statements about Abraham Lincoln* (Urbana: University of Illinois Press, 1998), 20–21; William H. Herndon and Jesse W.

Lincoln's love for Ann Rutledge, which historians generally agree was true, changed, however, from a simple doomed romance of young adults to the defining moment of Lincoln's life by Lincoln's law partner and later biographer, William Herndon. Herndon, who discovered the love affair while interviewing previous New Salem residents in the 1860s, called the courtship "the saddest page in Mr. Lincoln's history," and declared the memory of it "threw a melancholy shade over the remainder of his days."[2] Herndon contended that Lincoln never recovered from Ann's death, mourned her the rest of his life, never loved another woman and therefore suffered an unhappy marriage to Mary Todd because Mary could never match up to Ann's virtues.

As sociologist and historian Barry Schwartz has shown in his study of Ann Rutledge in American memory, through the late nineteenth and early twentieth centuries, the story of Abraham and Ann ultimately became one of the greatest love stories in American culture. It permeated poetry, fiction, biography, film, and drama, and, as the retellings grew, so did the depth and import of the romance itself.[3] The story eventually found its way to the pen of aspiring poet Edgar Lee Masters, who grew up in Beardstown, Illinois, only a few miles from New Salem. At the beginning of the twentieth century, Masters wrote what would become his masterpiece, *Spoon River Anthology*, a sequence of over two hundred free-verse poetic epitaphs spoken from the cemetery of the town of Spoon River. One of those epitaphs was of Ann Rutledge, who was not only Lincoln's true love but also the progenitor of his ultimate role as savior of the Union. "Out of me unworthy and unknown / The vibrations of deathless music," the twelve-line poem begins. "I am Ann Rutledge who sleep beneath these weeds, / Beloved in life of Abraham

---

Weik, *Herndon's Lincoln: The True Story of a Great Life*. Douglas L. Wilson and Rodney O. Davis, eds. (1889; repr. Urbana: University of Illinois Press, 2006), 90–91. For the only book-length examination of the Lincoln-Rutledge romance, see John Evangelist Walsh, *The Shadows Rise: Abraham Lincoln and the Ann Rutledge Legend* (Urbana: University of Illinois Press, 1993).

2. Herndon and Weik, *Herndon's Lincoln*, 89.

3. Barry Schwartz, "Ann Rutledge in American Memory: Social Change and the Erosion of a Romantic Drama," *Journal of the Abraham Lincoln Association* 26, no. 1 (Winter 2005): 1–27.

Lincoln, / Wedded to him, not through union, / But through separation. / Bloom forever, O Republic, / From the dust of my bosom!"[4]

Masters's poem (and book) has become a polestar of modern American poetry and, in 1921, the "eulogy" inscribed on Ann Rutledge's tombstone. The poem, however, has transcended poetry and become accepted history, with its grandiloquent pronouncements of true love and spiritual union being considered fact—to the detriment of Mary Lincoln. It was within this context that Iowa poet Martha Thomas Dyall, in 1937, wrote a poem about Mary Lincoln as her "answer" to Masters's Ann Rutledge poem.

Dyall was a homemaker and author who lived in Mt. Pleasant, Iowa. She loved to write both history and poetry, contributed numerous historical sketches to *The Palimpsest* of Iowa State Historical Society, published poems in journals and magazines and ultimately in a book titled *My House and Other Poems*. She belonged to numerous local, state, and national literary and historical organizations. In Dyall's 1942 obituary, it was said she "spent much of her time in writing and some of her poems had been published. She greatly enjoyed writing and found comfort and satisfaction in expressions both in prose and poetry."[5]

Coincidentally, Dyall's home of Mt. Pleasant was also the home of James Harlan, former U.S. senator, friend to President Abraham Lincoln, and father-in-law to the last living Lincoln son, Robert T. Lincoln. In fact, Robert's wife, Mary Harlan Lincoln, took their children—Mary "Mamie" (born in 1869), Abraham II "Jack" (born in 1872), and Jessie (born in 1875)—to visit her father in Mt. Pleasant multiple times every year and usually for many weeks throughout every summer. James Harlan and the Lincoln children were universally known and loved throughout the Mt. Pleasant community, and Dyall, who lived on the same street as the Harlan house, almost certainly was acquainted with them. When James Harlan died in 1899, Mary Harlan Lincoln inherited his house on North Main Street, and continued visiting Mt. Pleasant for a number of years afterward.

4. Edgar Lee Masters, *Spoon River Anthology* (1915; repr. N.Y.: Macmillan Company, 1921), 220.

5. "Mrs. Will Dyall Taken by Death," *Mt. Pleasant News*, Oct. 5, 1942; "Martha Thomas Dyall," *Who's Who in Iowa: A Biographical Record of Iowa's Leaders in Business, Professional and Public Life* (Iowa Press Association, 1940), 557.

In 1931, Dyall wrote an article for *The Palimpsest* titled "The Harlan Home," in which she described the home, the Harlan family, and the Lincoln family. She interviewed Mary Harlan Lincoln for the article. In 1938, Dyall, a member of the Iowa Federation of Women's Clubs, presented her original poem on Mary Todd Lincoln at the annual IFWC meeting in Des Moines in 1937. On January 3, 1938, she sent the poem and a letter to Jessie Lincoln Randolph, Robert and Mary's daughter, who was then living in Washington, D.C.[6]

The poem, as Dyall told Jessie Randolph, was a rebuttal to the Edgar Lee Masters's poem on Ann Rutledge, and a direct challenge to the notion that Ann Rutledge was more important than Mary Lincoln and that Abraham Lincoln never truly loved his wife.

❧

Mary Todd Lincoln

Under the towering marble
Erected to the memory of Abraham Lincoln,
I lie unnoticed in my crypt;
On the walls of which is the inscription:
"Mary Todd Lincoln, wife of Abraham Lincoln."
Yes, I, the wife of his bosom,
The mother of his sons,
His companion through life,
Holding him in my arms in death,
You pass me by and seek the grave on the hill
Where lies the girl you say he loved.
I ask you, is it fair—is it fair?

Martha Thomas Dyall

---

6. Mrs. Will Dyall to Jessie L. Randolph, Jan. 3, 1938, Folder 1938, Jessie Lincoln Papers Box 2, Robert Todd Lincoln Family Papers, Abraham Lincoln Presidential Library, Springfield, Illinois.

1940

Not all poems about Mary Lincoln were written by established poets or included in nationally published books. Some poets wrote about Mary just because they found her interesting, and some of their poems never were intended or expected to be published at all. One such instance of this occurred around Abraham Lincoln's 131st birthday in February 1940, when Mrs. Courtenay Fraser Fite, of Vicksburg, Mississippi, unknowingly found her poem, "The Spirit of Mary Todd Speaks," published in the February 18 issue of the *Jackson Daily News.*

"At a recent meeting of the Poetry Society I turned it in and did not know that it would be published," Mrs. Fite explained in a letter to Robert Todd Lincoln Beckwith, the great-grandson of Abraham Lincoln, who was at that time living in Chevy Chase, Maryland. "It is a custom to turn in poems at one meeting which are read at the next meeting so it happened I was not present at the reading but I am told it was favorably received. I had not heard of its publication when I wrote you yesterday or I would have enclosed it then."[1]

The meaning of Fite's poem is a bit difficult to comprehend, but basically it is the voice of Mary Lincoln from the spirit world explaining that although she was destined for criticism and hate during her time as Abraham Lincoln's wife and widow, she was happy to suffer "negation" to have been his love and allowed him to be "transcendent world light," admired by mankind.

1. Mrs. Courtenay Fraser Fite to Robert Todd Lincoln Beckwith, n.d., and newspaper clipping of poem, Lincoln Family Papers, Abraham Lincoln Presidential Library, Springfield, Ill.

The Spirit of Mary Todd Speaks

The spirit of Mary Todd speaks,
Born to Judas'-destiny, to world-hate,
In a less prejudiced day seeks
To stay disfavor's force, once great.

My acts were never my very own,
A controlled, determining power
Never left me unguided, alone,
But spaced the censored deed of each hour.

My Lincoln, transcendent world light,
Lifted high for man's emulation;
I, but an enveloping night,
Predestined to example negation.

But my chastened love became so great,
So infinite, humble, true,
I can bless the hand of fate
That stigmatized my name for you.

Courtenay Fraser Fite

1946

The Lincoln name is an institution in Springfield, Illinois, and every child reared there grows up inundated and permeated by the Lincoln legend. One such native son, Reed Miles Perkins, was born on March 1, 1875, while Mary Lincoln still was alive; he was a child of five when Mary returned to the town in 1880 to live her last years, and at age seven would have been aware of the immense funeral held for her during the summer of 1882. Perkins also had a direct connection to the Lincoln legend in that his father, Joseph B. Perkins, actually had known Abraham Lincoln (and possibly Mary). Joseph not only lived in Springfield but also served for a time as the sheriff, and in 1859 he was sued by a man whose legal counsel was the firm of Lincoln & Herndon.

Reed Perkins graduated from the University of Illinois in 1898 and Illinois Wesleyan in 1902. He trained as a lawyer, his profession was as a merchant (he was proprietor of the Perkins Ice & Coal Company from 1902–1914, and later the manager of Perkins Bros. Cattle farm), but his passion was poetry.[1] He published three books of verse, but it was in his first, *Prairie Poems* (1946), that his fascination with the Lincolns was explored and versified. In addition to poems on Abraham Lincoln, Stephen A. Douglas, and the Old State House where Lincoln practiced politics, Perkins also penned a sonnet for Mary Lincoln in which he admired her as loving wife and helpful mate.

1. Franklin W. Scott, ed., *Semi-Centennial Alumni Record of the University of Illinois* (University of Illinois, 1918), 114.

Mary Todd Lincoln

She left her sheltered home in old Kentucky
To merge her life with an aspiring mate;
Ambitious, cultured, persevering, plucky,
She helped him upward to his high estate.
She saw this woodsman from the Salem clearing,
Coarse-barked and knotty, schooled in rude debate,
With polished style beyond her own proud rearing,
Command a diction that enthralled the state.

She made his home and watched his constant growing;
Encouraged when the debris blocked the way;
She cherished all the glory he was knowing,
And kept alive ambition day by day.
At last his life-blood left its tragic stain
Upon her dress and on her weary brain.

Reed Miles Perkins

Carmichael was profoundly moved by the Civil War, about which she wrote numerous dramatic poems, including her best-known poem, "President Lincoln's Funeral." This elegy attracted national attention, was reprinted in newspapers across the country, and read many times at public functions. The poem not only included sentiments for the widowed first lady, but also reportedly was greatly admired by Mary Lincoln for its "solemn dignity."[3]

⚜

President Lincoln's Funeral

Toll! Toll!
Toll! Toll!
All rivers seaward wend.
Toll! Toll!
Toll! Toll!
Weep for the nation's friend.

Every home and hall was shrouded,
Every thoroughfare was still;
Every brow was darkly clouded,
Every heart was faint and chill.
Oh! the inky drop of poison
In our bitter draught of grief!
Oh! the sorrow of a nation
Mourning for its murdered chief!

Toll! Toll!
Toll! Toll!
Bound is the reaper's sheaf—
Toll! Toll!

3. Sarah E. Carmichael, *Poems* (Utah, 1866), 21–24; Miriam B. Murphy, "Sarah Elizabeth Carmichael: Poetic Genius of Pioneer Utah," *Utah Historical Quarterly* 43, no. 1 (Winter 1975): 52–66.

1955

The theme of the poetry about Mary Lincoln in the first half of the twentieth century focused on her loving place at her husband's side; but it was not until Jane Merchant's 1955 poem about Mary that the Lincolns were written as a true love story.

Merchant was born in 1919, the youngest of four children, on a dairy farm outside Knoxville, Tennessee. She was confined to her bed at age twelve due to the congenital bone disease *osteogenesis imperfecta,* which made her bones extremely brittle and prevented virtually all physical activity, including going to school. It also caused her to go deaf at the age of twenty-three. What little of the outside world Jane saw was from her parents' arms when they carried her outside as a child.

Merchant refused to be hindered by her physical condition, and was active in literary circles her entire life, including carrying on a worldwide correspondence with other authors and literati. She became a prolific writer of more than 3,000 poems, over 2,000 letters, dozens of prose pieces, and ten published collections of poetry. Her book, *The Greatest of These* (1954), received the Best Book of Poetry award from the National League of American Pen Women, and she was awarded the Beaudoin Gemstone Award for Poetry in 1965. She died in 1972.[1]

Merchant's poem, "Valentine for Mary Lincoln," is a panegyric written for a woman whom the poet saw as admirable yet misunderstood. It was pub-

1. For the life of Jane Merchant, see Sarah Ricketts, *A Window on Eternity: The Life and Poetry of Jane Hess Merchant* (Nashville: Abingdon Press, 1989).

lished in the *Washington Star* newspaper on Valentine's Day 1955. Merchant told historian Ruth Painter Randall that her inspiration came after reading Randall's 1953 book, *Mary Lincoln: Biography of a Marriage*. Randall, who believed and often wrote that Mary Lincoln's reputation had been wrongly maligned, later reprinted Merchant's poem in her children's book about Mary Lincoln, stating, "The very fact that such a poem has been written is a heartwarming sign that at last justice to Mary has been done."[2]

Valentine for Mary Lincoln

Forgive us, Mary, for the cruel lies
   We long believed of you; that you were only
A nagging burden to the patient, wise,
   Great-hearted man who bore the anguished, lonely
Weight of a warring nation. We have thought
   You gave him little help or tenderness
And with self-centered, angry tempers brought
   More sorrow to him in his great distress.
We have grown wiser now; we know you gave
   Him love and understanding without measure,
And were warm-hearted, kind, and deeply brave—
   I write you this to tell you that we treasure
Your memory; and most of all, to tell
You that we know, at last, he loved you well.

Jane Merchant

2. Ruth Painter Randall, *I, Mary: A Biography of the Girl Who Married Abraham Lincoln* (Boston: Little, Brown & Co., 1959), acknowledgements, 219–20.

1965

For more than half a century after President Lincoln's death, Mary Lincoln was seen and considered more as Abraham's wife than as her own person. Historians seeking facts or opinions about Mary, therefore, often were—and still are—forced to scour pages of biographies of the Great Emancipator if they wanted to learn facts about his wife. The search for poetry about Mary Lincoln is no different.

A pleasant trove of nearly one dozen poems concerning Mary Lincoln is contained in a truly astonishing three-volume life of Lincoln published in 1965, and written completely in verse. The author, Della Crowder Miller, spent nine years on her biography in sonnet sequence because she felt that sonnets were the "highest form of literature," and because a love of poetry was such a part of Lincoln's life.[1]

Any poet who has attempted a sonnet knows the difficulty of its construction, especially if it is done correctly. Miller's history is accurate, while the feelings, tone, and settings she describes are well done.[2] The poems themselves, while an impressive total feat, are rather pedestrian—meant more for imparting information than for inspiring with high language and

1. Della Crowder Miller, *Abraham Lincoln: A Biographic Treatment in Sonnet Sequence*, 3 vols. (Boston: Christopher Publishing House, 1965), 1:xix. Miller's biography contains many varieties of sonnet forms, but the majority are Petrarchan.

2. Lincoln scholar Allan Nevins called Miller's poetry, "fluent, polished, and most interesting." Miller, *Abraham Lincoln*, 1:xxvi.

soaring emotion. Miller's poems concerning Mary Lincoln certainly are not the most impressive in impact or provocation in the canon, although they are worthwhile.

Throughout Miller's three-volume work, a number of poems specifically focus on Mary Lincoln, while numerous others mention Mary secondarily. Two of Miller's poems have been included here, chosen for their poetic accomplishments and their historical subject matter. The first of the two poems, "Mary Visits Lexington: 1848–1849," concerns the time when Mary took sons Robert and Eddie to the Todd home in Lexington while Congressman Abraham Lincoln worked in Washington. The family had traveled to Washington together, but after a few months Mary felt lonely and contained within the boardinghouse, while Lincoln felt that his family's presence was getting in the way of his congressional work.

The first stanza of the poem is a reference to the bad manners and behaviors of the Lincoln boys. They were famous hellions (especially younger two sons Willie and Tad), and lodgers at Mrs. Ann G. Sprigg's boardinghouse in Washington where the Lincoln family stayed were glad to be rid of the rascals (Robert and Eddie at that time) when they left in early spring 1848. Both Mary and Abraham Lincoln had the parenting philosophy to let the boys do as they pleased, and they reveled in their children's happiness.[3] Of course to other adults, the boys were just spoiled brats. One of Mrs. Sprigg's boarders, Dr. Samuel C. Busey, remembered, rather critically, that four-year-old Robert "seemed to have his own way."[4] The second stanza of Miller's poem refers to the love letters between Mary and Abraham during their separation.[5]

---

3. According to Mary Lincoln, her husband liked to say, "It is my pleasure that my children are free, happy and unrestrained by parental tyranny." Mary Lincoln, interview by William Herndon, Wilson and Davis, *Herndon's Informants,* 357.

4. Samuel C. Busey, M.D., LL.D., *Personal Reminiscences and Recollections of Forty-Six Years' Membership in the Medical Society of the District of Columbia, and Residence in This City* (Philadelphia: Dornan, Printer, 1895), 28.

5. See "1848," page 7.

Mary Visits Lexington: 1848–1849

The Lincoln children had small discipline,
For winsome Mary held a selfish creed:
"Oh, let them have their way!" She failed to heed
their trespassing on others' rights with din
That brought confusion, and to some, chagrin.
Her father wrote to urge her meet a need
By coming as his guest. This did indeed
Bring joy and peace to lodgers at the inn.

How much the Lincolns felt their loneliness,
Apart, is shown by letters which they penned;
Not one is left but breathes its love caress.
And all the while, Abe seemed to apprehend
Forebodings that were given added stress
In statements proving true love has no end.

Della Crowder Miller

1965

The second of Della Crowder Miller's poems included here concerns Mary Lincoln's social tribulations. As first lady during the Civil War, Mary had a difficult time in the White House as the country's—and the capital city's—leader of society. She was expected to be the exemplar of fashion and entertainment, and yet every time she bought a dress, redecorated the (dilapidated) White House, or hosted a ball, she was mercilessly criticized for purchasing or celebrating in time of war. Simultaneously, if she canceled an entertainment or appeared in a dress more than once, she was criticized for not doing her social duties.

Washington female society also disliked Mary Lincoln for her origins and attitudes. They openly scoffed at her as an uncouth westerner—which she was not—and attempted to direct her conduct, which the proud Mary openly resented. Many in Washington also scoffed at Mary's sense of regal entitlement and often haughty air.[1] Also difficult was the criticism from Northerners that she was some kind of rebel traitor, since she was from Kentucky; while Southerners considered her a southern traitor, because she supported her Republican husband. And then there was simple jealousy

---

1. For examples of Mary Lincoln's societal relations and actions, see Horatio Taft, diary entries for Jan. 2, 1863, and Dec. 14, 1864, in John R. Sellers, ed., *Washington During the Civil War: The Diary of Horatio Nelson Taft, 1861–1865*, 3 vols., Manuscripts Division, Library of Congress. Published online, Feb. 12, 2002, www.memory.loc.gov; Willis Steell, "Mrs. Abraham Lincoln and Her Friends," *Munsey's Magazine* 40, no. 5 (Feb. 1909): 617–23; Virginia Kinnaird, "Mrs. Lincoln as a White House Hostess," *Papers in Illinois History and Transactions for the Year 1938* (Springfield: Illinois State Historical Society, 1939), 65–87.

from numerous quarters who all thought themselves better qualified to be first lady. As biographer Ruth Painter Randall declared, "Few women have been placed in as difficult and lonely a position as Mrs. Lincoln."[2]

❧

Mrs. Lincoln Given Social Snubs: October, 1861

The White House decorating had been done,
Including floors, gas fixtures and the walls;
And when the social season opened, halls
And rooms were ready for display. Each one
Who previously perceived the welcome change and none
But felt an admiration that enthralls.
The dates had now been set for two grand balls,
And Mary Lincoln's gowns were all begun.

Since custom had decreed a White House tea
Should not be closed against the public's will,
Her holding of a *private* coterie
Soon brought resentment from the social mill;
And leaders stayed at home, to make her see
Her action gained democracy's keen chill.

Della Crowder Miller

2. Randall, *Mary Lincoln: Biography of a Marriage* (Boston: Little, Brown and Company, 1953), 216.

1987

Probably the most dramatic and fascinating event in Mary Lincoln's life was her commitment to a sanitarium in May 1875. As far back as 1865, Mary's family and friends, as well as members of the general public and the news media, had been saying that Mary was not mentally stable— although, unlike modern biographies that shun this talk as personal attacks against Mary, back then the general consensus was: Her husband was murdered right in front of her; who would not go insane?

Mary suffered numerous symptoms of mental disease, including severe depression, auditory hallucinations (she often heard voices in the walls and the floors of her room), visual hallucinations (Mary told her doctor an Indian ghost was removing and replacing her scalp, pulling the wires out of her eyes and the bones out of her jaw, to which he testified in court), and a monomania for shopping (she purchased trunkloads full of items she never used nor wore, just stored them away and spent hours every day unpacking and repacking them in her trunks).

After years of watching his mother's bizarre and erratic behavior, Robert Lincoln, Mary's oldest and only surviving son who practiced law in Chicago, had his mother declared insane by a group of doctors, and, ultimately, a Chicago jury. She was sent to Bellevue Place sanitarium, a private asylum in Batavia, Illinois, where she stayed for four months. While there, Robert visited his mother every week, sometimes bringing with him his daughter Mamie, whom Grandmother Lincoln adored. Mary spent the remaining eight months of her court-declared "insanity" living with her sister and brother-in-law, Elizabeth and Ninian Edwards, at their Springfield, Illinois, home. Mary was declared "restored to reason" by a second Chicago jury in June 1876.[1]

A watershed moment concerning the history—and therefore the poetry—of Mary Lincoln occurred in the late twentieth century with the publication of two books offering new facts and interpretations on Mary's insanity case: *The Insanity File: The Case of Mary Todd Lincoln*, by Mark E. Neely and R. Gerald McMurtry (1986), and *Mary Todd Lincoln: A Biography*, by Jean H. Baker (1987). The former was the first book ever published dedicated solely to an examination of Mary Lincoln's commitment; the latter was the first biography of Mary published in thirty years and has since become the preeminent biography of the Civil War first lady.

Both books opened a new door into Mary's life and brought her insanity case to the forefront of history for the first time. For the next nearly twenty years, the theme of insanity would dominate poetic interpretations of Mary Lincoln. The first of these was by Edward C. Lynskey with his poem "Mrs. Lincoln Enters Bellevue Place," published in *College English* in December 1987. This is the first of Lynskey's five poems about Mary Lincoln written and published between 1987 and 2002. Of these five, two have been included here, both of which concern Mary's mental health and stay at Bellevue Place sanitarium.

---

1. For complete examinations of the insanity episode and case, see Jason Emerson, *The Madness of Mary Lincoln* (Carbondale: Southern Illinois University Press), 2007, and Mark E. Neely and R. Gerald McMurtry, *The Insanity File: The Case of Mary Todd Lincoln* (Carbondale: Southern Illinois University Press), 1986.

🌿

Mrs. Lincoln Enters Bellevue Place

Ten o'clock Pliny Earle my own physician
administers chloral drops, then the Indian
ghost returns to lift my scalp and unhook
again the banjo strings behind my eyes.
When I hear other voices trapped between
the walls, the quack scribbles in his ledger:

a debility of the nervous system. Rest
comes when I dream of wintering this year
quietly among the limes and oranges, left
alone to concentrate my mind wonderfully,
embracing the kiss of kin as if still near.
It is the drudgery of this modern management

of mental disease by morphia, ale, croquet,
monitored menstrual flow and fresh air I so
long to divorce. Ninety sleepy miles by
freight from Chicago, Robert visits on a lawyer's
Wednesday afternoons when we walk, arms linked,

in the yellow wood. He brings me crinoline,
grieves I suspect for not taking me, but our
little experiment caused him to break housekeeping
to end the troubles I brewed with his wife. At night
when the moon falls in bars across my pillow, I think
of all those white gloves locked in trunks and smile.

Edward C. Lynskey

Bellevue Place Sanitarium, Batavia, Illinois. Mary Lincoln spent four months undergoing medical treatment here in 1875 after a Chicago jury declared her insane. Courtesy Batavia Historical Society, Batavia, Illinois.

1997

M ary Lincoln's stay at Bellevue Place was not harsh but pleasant, even privileged. Mary had complete freedom of the grounds and buildings, typically took her meals with the doctor and his family, and could even travel to nearby towns as long as she was accompanied by an attendant. Her physician, Dr. R. J. Patterson, practiced "moral therapy," which consisted of healthy dieting, daily exercise, diverting the mind through activities (specifically gardening), frequent bathing, talking with the medical staff, and no medications unless absolutely necessary.[1]

Robert Lincoln, who visited his mother once a week at Bellevue Place, believed his mother's time at the sanitarium helped her; and his actions were nearly universally lauded across the United States at the time. Jean Baker's 1987 biography of Mary Lincoln, however, painted the son as a heartless, avaricious, misogynistic scoundrel who bribed the judge and jury in order to shut away his mother so he could steal her money. Although Baker's statements and conclusions about Robert Lincoln's character, motivations, and actions are believed by most Lincoln scholars to be entirely distorted and incorrect, they continue to be the dominant interpretation, including in the following poem by Edward Lynskey, originally published in *Commonweal* in June 1997.

---

1. For detailed descriptions of Bellevue Place sanitarium when Mary was a resident, see Emerson, *The Madness of Mary Lincoln*, 71–73, and "Mrs. Lincoln: A Visit to Her by 'The Post and Mail' Correspondent: How She Passes the Time at Dr. Patterson's Retreat," *Chicago Post and Mail*, July 13, 1875.

Mrs. Lincoln's Epistle from Bellevue Place

At lamplighting the Indian maid Little
Pinkie slinks under a prairie dog moon
to tie up my wits end. What now? More
morphia? Yes, that's the solution made
famous in your "Hospital for the Insane
of the Private Class." I'll never dip
my quill pen deep down a poisoned ink phial

to spell out my soul's sores for Matron
to clutch up to a candle, poring over my
sentences to hang me, Mary the Madwoman.
Robert whistles up on the Electric Express
in his shyster's swank for our promenade.
Chicago's moiling gales subvert his cheer.
I mew, "Life's a bed of roses." He rasps

"I abhor the night." Before sun-go-down
he's gone. "She dons gloves for repast,"
Dr. Pliny Elder scribbles in his ledger.
Crochet again today? Chinaman's marbles
tonight? Red rice tomorrow? Tally ho!
"Come here," I murmur to my mate recalled
by the door, "Lay your bones inside mine."

Edward C. Lynskey

1999

L ike the numerous mischaracterizations of Robert Lincoln in regard to his mother's insanity case, the conditions in which Mary lived at the sanitarium have been largely misrepresented or misunderstood. Bellevue Place was a nationally respected private asylum for "a select class of lady patients of quiet unexceptionable habits." Typical patients—of whom there were twenty during Mary's stay—were nervous invalids who were not insane, but "who occupy a border-land between undoubted insanity and doubtful sanity," and incurable patients who either could not gain admission to state hospitals, or whose families preferred a more private retreat. The majority of patients were depressed, some were suicidal, but all were quiet, as Dr. Patterson did not admit patients who were noisy, violent, or destructive.[1]

Unlike how Mary Lincoln is represented in the following poem, "Mary Lincoln on Her Deathbed," by Julianna Baggott,[2] the former first lady was not surrounded by raving maniacs during her time at the sanitarium; she was surrounded by quiet women who were mentally unwell. What is true

1. For descriptions of Bellevue Place and its patients, see Bellevue Place Sanitarium Advertising Brochures, n.d., 2 pages, and 1895, 15 pages, Batavia Historical Society, Batavia, Illinois; "Mrs. Lincoln: A Visit to Her by 'The Post and Mail' Correspondent," *Chicago Post and Mail*, July 13, 1875; Rodney Ross, "Mary Todd Lincoln, Patient at Bellevue Place," *Journal of the Illinois State Historical Society*, 63, no. 1 (Spring 1970): 5–34.

2. Originally published in *Quarterly West* 48, (Spring/Summer 1999): 34–35. Reprinted in *Best American Poetry 2000*, and in Baggott, *Lizzie Borden in Love: Poems in Women's Voices*, Crab Orchard Series in Poetry (Carbondale: Southern Illinois University Press, 2006), 17–18.

in this poem is the reference to the "tireless Jew who wore me down."
During Mary's train ride from Jacksonville, Florida, to Chicago in March
1875, when she was rushing to her oldest son Robert, whom she mistakenly
was convinced was dying, Mary believed that a "Wandering Jew" had been
following her and had taken her pocketbook but would return it to her "at
3 o'clock." Mary thought the strange man had poisoned her coffee on the
train, as she told her doctor, to which he testified at her insanity hearing.

This poem is an interesting representation of Mary's thoughts while in
the asylum because it portrays what is evident in Mary's own letters: that
she spent much of her time at Bellevue Place reflecting on her life, the loss
of her husband and three children, and the situation she found herself in
due to the actions of her oldest child.

Mary Todd on Her Deathbed

I can hear them, choking on spoons, screaming
in shower stalls; the fat are given only
a raw egg and whiskey
    and those who refuse to eat
are force-fed. The least crazy sing,
picking scalp scabs in window seats.
One woman finds scissors
    and stabs herself
again and again. It was the tireless Jew
who wore me down; no one believed
that he followed me
    from train to train
with his satchel of poisons, sneering
as they searched my baggage
for the stolen hotel footstools, how he knew
that I shuffled because my petticoats,
stitched so tight with money,
    had become a heavy net

for dredging the lost. And I do not speak of the lost:
Abe could have worn me as a boutonniere,
my pinched face, say it: an ugly plump bud,
hoisted skirts and petticoats
   the leaf and ribbon trim.
I remember the hoisted skirts,
how his body seemed
   a long white country of its own.
But it was owned by a country
of citizens as unruly as my dead boys,
my dead boys
   roaring through the White House.
Nothing was mine, after all. Strangers
crowded his open coffin, snipped souvenirs
from the curtains,
    slipped hands
into the casket to unclip his cufflinks.
All the while, they could hear me
     wailing from bed.
Every day I can move slightly less;
each body hinge becomes more stubborn
    than memory.
I know how I will die: a clenched jaw,
fists gripping bed sheets. Stiff with longing,
I will have to break
   into heaven, the willows
in my handmade girlhood hoop-skirt snapping.

Julianna Baggott

2003

A major turning point in Mary Lincoln's life occurred with the death of her eleven-year-old son Willie in February 1862. Willie Lincoln was a precocious, honest, kind, and thoughtful boy—the inheritor of all his father's best traits. He was a great reader and lover of books, especially poetry, just like his parents; he even composed an original poem on the death of his father's good friend, Edward Baker in 1861.[1] Willie was loved and admired by all who knew him, and is considered to have been his parents' favorite son.

In early 1862, Willie (and his younger brother Tad) contracted typhoid fever from polluted drinking water. He was ill for nearly three weeks, confined to his bed, worried over by his parents. Mary Lincoln had scheduled a grand White House ball for the night of February 5 and, because Willie appeared to be improving, did not cancel it. As the festivities went on downstairs in the White House that night, the president and first lady continuously left the party to check on their sick boy. On February 20, Willie died.

"He was so bravely and beautifully himself," eulogized poet and family friend N. P. Willis. "A wild flower, transplanted from the prairie to the hothouse, he retained his prairie habits, unalterably pure and simple, till he died."[2]

---

1. Baker was killed at the Battle of Ball's Bluff in Oct. 1861. The poem was published in the Washington *National Republican*, Nov. 4, 1861, 1, and also reprinted in Keckley, *Behind the Scenes*, 99–100. (See introduction, note 12.)

2. N. P. Willis, "The President's Son," *Littell's Living Age* 933 (April 19, 1862): 154.

Both the Lincolns were devastated by the loss. Mary, similar to her reaction when her four-year-old son Eddie had died in 1850, was inconsolable. She stayed confined to her room for weeks, and could not look at anything connected with her darling boy. Mary's seamstress, Elizabeth Keckley, later recalled that in the midst of one of Mary's paroxysms of grief, "the President kindly bent over his wife, took her by the arm, and gently led her to a window. With a stately, solemn gesture, he pointed to the lunatic asylum. 'Mother, do you see that large white building on the hill yonder? Try and control your grief, or it will drive you mad, and we may have to send you there.'"[3]

Mary's half sister, Emilie Todd Helm, noticed during a stay in the White House in 1863 that Mary still was grappling with her grief over Willie's death. Emilie recorded in her diary a most disturbing event in which Mary came into her room one night, smiling and with eyes full of tears, to tell her that Willie visited her at night: "'He lives Emilie!' she said with a thrill in her voice I can never forget. 'He comes to me every night, and stands at the foot of my bed with the same sweet, adorable smile he always had; he does not always come alone; little Eddie is sometimes with him and twice he has come with our brother Alec,[4] he tells me he loves his Uncle Alec and is with him most of the time. You cannot dream of the comfort this gives me. When I thought of my little son in immensity, alone, without his mother to direct him, no one to hold his little hand in loving guidance, it nearly broke my heart.' Sister Mary's eyes were wide and shining and I had the feeling of awe as if I were in the presence of the supernatural. It *is* unnatural and abnormal, it frightens me."[5]

In the following poem Laurence Overmire, a lover of history who is popularly known as "The Genealogist-Poet," sympathetically explores Mary's feelings in the aftermath of her beloved son's death.[6]

---

3. Keckley, *Behind the Scenes*, 104–5.
4. Alexander Todd, Mary's youngest brother, died serving with the Confederate army during a skirmish at Baton Rouge, La., in August 1862.
5. Helm, *True Story of Mary*, 227.
6. Previously published on Ancestry.com, 2003.

Willie at the Foot of the Bed
(An Ode to Mary Todd Lincoln)

Every night he comes, Mary
Do you see him?

Smiling as he did before
No pain in those forgiving eyes

Can he put your mind to rest?
Give you comfort in these terrible times?

A world gone mad
The thunder of guns pounding in the brain

Fires burning, men running, screaming
Limbs falling, hand and foot, out of the sky

Blood oozing in rivulets from the sodden ground
This nightmare we dream together

Why can't we will it, ever to end?
Pull the bed sheets close, Mary

Willie, take your mother's hand
Your father weeps outside the door

And the night, so long and cold
May never end.

Laurence Overmire

2006

One of the great constants of human existence is war, as is the suffering that accompanies it. The Civil War remains the touchstone in American memory; and Mary Lincoln's suffering because of that war likewise remains a historical measuring stick for human affliction and endurance. She lost her son, her husband, and numerous family members and friends, and the losses devastated her. Her lifelong spells of depression came on stronger and longer; her normal love of shopping and spending money deteriorated into an unreasonable mania for possessions she neither used nor wore—inanimate possessions that could never die nor ever leave her.

Mary's behaviors during and after the war, which many considered bizarre and ultimately insane, were not unique to her, especially not in wartime. And while she most likely did suffer some sort of mental illness, who could not then—or cannot today—understand her position and empathize with her trials and tribulations? It is within this juxtaposition of war and suffering, as seen through the perspective of Mary Lincoln, that Kathleen Flenniken composed the following poem.[1]

---

1. Originally published in the *Iowa Review* 34, no. 2 (Fall 2004): 76; reprinted in Flenniken, *Famous* (Lincoln: University of Nebraska Press, 2006): 69–70.

To Ease My Mind

If I woke as Mary Todd Lincoln

and if Abraham Lincoln slept next to me
like an uprooted tree, his knobby fingers

unearthed, his face a burl,
grey as a Mathew Brady photograph,

and if my country were at war,

my own cousins killing my cousins,
and I'd been told to tear the country's

damask down, shred its opulence
to bandage the wounded but

I knew it was hopeless, hopeless,
there'd be no stopping the blood

of filthy, putrid common men until
every human left had lost a child, a leg, an arm

and if I'd already given everything,

if I'd given over my grieving husband—
not without kicking and screaming—

and the birds were silent
to mark the never-ending end,

then God forgive me, perhaps I too
would turn my mind to the pleasures

of kidskin gloves adorned with pearls,
embroidered daisies and chrysanthemum

stars, white on white filigree so fine
one might believe a fairy tatted them.

I might need box upon box upon box of them
to tell me who I am.

Kathleen Flenniken

2007

The Abraham Lincoln-Mary Todd courtship, which began in 1839, was passionate and ultimately tumultuous. They were attracted to each other for numerous reasons, including a shared love of children, Whig politics, poetry, and literature. They both, in fact, loved reading books of all types, and often read aloud to each other during their courtship and throughout their marriage.

In 1840 the couple decided to wed, but at the end of that year Lincoln broke the engagement, feeling himself unworthy and unqualified to make such a woman from an aristocratic background happy in a middle-class life. The break plunged Lincoln into a fit of melancholy for which he received medical treatment; and he later dubbed the day of the break "that fatal first of January."[1]

The couple resumed their relationship eighteen months later, meeting secretly at a mutual friend's home to avoid censure or criticism, especially from Mary's disapproving family. Abraham and Mary decided hastily to marry on the evening of November 4, 1842, giving only hours of advance notice to family and friends. The cake, in fact, still was warm when it was served after the ceremony. At the altar that day Lincoln gave his bride a ring with the inscription "A.L. to Mary, Nov. 4, 1842: Love is Eternal."

1. There are numerous articles and book chapters that examine the story of the Lincoln-Todd courtship, broken engagement, and wedding. For two of the best, see Mary Leighton Miles, "'The Fatal First of January, 1841,'" *Journal of the Illinois State Historical Society* 20, no. 1 (April 1927): 13–48; and Douglas L. Wilson, "Abraham Lincoln and 'That Fatal First of January,'" *Civil War History*, 38, no. 2 (June 1992): 101–30.

Historians continue to debate whether the Lincoln marriage was a loving one with typical ups and downs, or whether Abraham Lincoln lived in a veritable hell inhabited by a termagant wife who drove him out of the house and therefore into political greatness. Poet Dan Guillory, in his book, *The Lincoln Poems,* [2] takes the former view of the Lincolns, as shown with gusto in the following two selections.

"Love Is Eternal"—November 4, 1842

Sweet Mary, I am schoolboy at your side, student
Of the bound volume abundant with information.
The theme, the meaning develops as a series
Of impressions under my fingertips.
A little crease here, some dog-eared flap—
Gently thumbing the well-tooled spine.
There is reassurance in the familiar—
Sadness at the inevitable ending.
And perfect pleasure, reading it again
As if for the very first time.

Dan Guillory

2. Guillory, *The Lincoln Poems* (Mahomet, Ill.: Mayhaven Publishing, 2007).

Mary Todd Lincoln as a young woman, portrait by Lloyd Ostendorf, 1980.
Courtesy of Mary Todd Lincoln House, Lexington, Kentucky.

2007

Throughout her life, Mary Lincoln was famous for her headstrong ways, her impulsive buying habits, and her tempestuous temper. But her life was never easy, with a husband gone circuit riding for more than half the year while she struggled to keep house and raise four boys, two of whom were dead before the end of President Lincoln's first term in office.

For all the ups and downs of their relationship, poet Dan Guillory believes Lincoln was deeply and passionately attracted to Mary throughout his life. It is known Abraham had numerous pet names for his wife such as "Molly," "Puss," "child wife," and "little woman"; although after the birth of their first son, Robert, Lincoln usually called his wife "Mother."

During the Civil War, numerous people witnessed and later testified to the warmth and love between the president and first lady. General Daniel Sickles, who knew the Lincolns on a personal level, stated he had "never seen a more devoted couple," while abolitionist Jane Grey Swisshelm noted their devotion in the way that Mary "completely merged herself in her husband."[1] One friend later recalled how much Abraham "clearly loved" his wife, and remembered him during a White House ball, observing his wife, laughing pleasantly, and saying, "My wife is as handsome as when she was a girl, and I, a poor nobody then, fell in love with her; and what is more, I have never fallen out."[2]

1. Helm, *True Story of Mary*, 195; Swisshelm, "Tribute to the Dead," *Chicago Tribune*, July 20, 1882, 7.

2. C. E. L., "A Kindly Word for Abraham Lincoln's Widow," *The Christian Register* 101, no. 36 (September 7, 1872): 1.

Litany for Mary T.

O, terrible She
Angel-fat goddess
My tormenting Daemon
In black-toed slippers
My dancing accordion.

She of the seven petticoats
And the slit-open drawers,
Eyes fierce as a lynx
Nakedness all musk and mink.

O, she of the burning gaze
The upcurled lip
The little finger
Hooked behind my ear
That hitching-post of love,

She of the marble knees
The alabaster throat
The breasts of cool pink jade
Nippled in coral.

She of the half-drunk goblet
And the fluted white napkin.
She of the proper fork
And fluent French phrase.

She of the endless purse—
Pillager of millinery shops,
Jewelry and cutlery
Copper silver gold
Brooches pearls pins

Necklaces bracelets gems
Flimsy tulle veils whalebone
Corsets and lacework shawls.

She of the meaty jowls
Eater of roasts and Virginia hams
Candied yams blackberry cobbler
Cool tumblers of buttermilk

Brushing white her hirsute lip.
She of the serpent's tongue
It uncoils with a kiss
Slithers into your mouth
Where the venom
Turned everything into a Lie.
She of the comet-bright hair
With darkly-tufted underarms
The ineffable furrow
Unspeakable furze and fat
Portal of heaven
Gate of Hell.

O, she of the buttery bellyfat
The small tendrils of lust
The pungent crevices
The fermenting dark fruit
Where I am drunken nocturnal fool
Voracious and never satisfied.

Dan Guillory

2007

One of Mary Lincoln's lesser-known characteristics during her life in Springfield was her intense fear of thunderstorms, especially if they occurred when her husband was not at home. Mary was terrified of the noise and the danger of the house being struck by lightning and catching fire. As storms approached, or struck without warning, Abraham Lincoln would rush the few blocks from his downtown law office to his home to comfort his shivering wife until the storm passed. According to one witness, Mary, knowing her husband would come, "would meet him at their gate just a step from their front door, where his protecting arm would be slipped into hers, and so arm in arm they would go into the house together."[1]

Mary Lincoln's life of fear and suffering, of relentless sorrows, has drawn numerous writers, historians, and artists to her story. California poet Michael Meng has, in fact, written a book-length anthology of poems on the Civil War first lady.[2] The following two selections of Meng's work show his empathy and compassion for a woman whom he believes deserves a greater understanding of the complex circumstances of her life.

1. Helm, *True Story of Mary*, 120; Randall, *Mary Lincoln*, 118–19.
2. *The Dark Lily: A Commemorative Poetry for the Life and Times of Mary Todd Lincoln*, currently unpublished.

The Foreshadowing

When the clouds gathered to do their mischief,
When the portent of their design affixed itself upon the firmament,
Mary was given to fits of trembling fear.

As the heavens stirred in blackness,
As bolts of lightning struck and flashed above,
Mary cried aloud for him.

On through the pitch of morn he came,
Long urgent strides across the square,
Racing up the street where love, forlorn, was waiting.

At the gate she cringed.
In the rocking of heaven there was no answer.

But the man whose hand was slipped,
Whose long, great arm was made a linchpin of love,
Taking hold inside her heart, lifting her, relieved in the cradling
     peace
That banished fume and roar and myth of discordant heavens.

Michael Meng

2007

Mary Lincoln was overjoyed in November 1860 when her husband was elected president of the United States. She not only loved him but had an abiding belief in his great abilities, and an ambition for his political success as unrelenting as his own. She reveled in her new position as first lady of the land, and was eminently qualified for it. She was educated, intelligent, witty, charming, with excellent conversational skills, dancing skills, entertaining skills, and fashion sense.

In the four months between the election and the inauguration, countless journalists who met Mary found her impressive and likeable, and predicted for her a marvelous social reign in Washington. Mary, too, knew she would fill her position with grace and dignity. The outbreak of war, however, changed the entire dynamic of the Lincolns' residence in the White House. Had there been no war, Mary may have become the most admired and respected first lady in American history; but her fragile emotions and quick temperament could not withstand the myriad criticisms poured upon a wartime administration.

Yet, on the day of her husband's inauguration, and at the inaugural ball that night, Mary Lincoln shone like a sunbeam on a cloudy day. She wore that evening a spectacular low-necked, blue watered silk gown, trimmed with lace; was adorned in pearls on throat, ears, and wrists; and wore a blue ostrich feather and roselike camellias in her hair. Her exquisite toilet was admired by everyone in the room, and the *New York Times* applauded the new first lady as "evidently a lady of refinement, of tact and of taste."[1]

---

1. Donna McCreary, *Fashionable First Lady: The Victorian Wardrobe of Mary Lincoln* (Carmel, Ind.: Lincoln Presentations, 2007), 30.

First Lady Mary Lincoln pictured in one of her many ball gowns. This picture is believed to have been taken in January 1862. Courtesy Library of Congress Prints and Photographs Division, Washington, D.C.

Mary Todd Lincoln in Her Inaugural Ball Gown

In lovely stripes
That streamed across a ballroom floor,

Lincoln's lady danced with love.

She was garbed in rapture's cloth,
Swirling in a world growing dim.

As her bodice draped her shoulders 'round,
Every bit of lace about them sung of woman loved,
And all the worldly fabric donning,
Fairly wrapped,

Around the man for whom she bore.

She would,
Like so many other lovelies taken,
Hide inside her princess clothes
And dream a world all her own,

That men would find soon forsaken.

But this night,
I saw her in the beauty of a necklace caught,
In the pierce of spiral rings,
Crowned with pastel flowers,
Alight a nest of chestnut hair.

Lincoln's lady was only of a world
That would be lost to war.

But for just one night at least,
Her one and only man,
Who wanted her to have the world she loved,

Would sweep her off her earthbound feet,
And give her mind the sweetest taste

Of what she thought was heaven.

Michael Meng

2008

One of the enduring stories about Abraham Lincoln was the omen of his death he supposedly saw and later described to a journalist. Shortly after receiving news of his election to the presidency in November 1860, Lincoln, exhausted from the long day of waiting for results, went home and threw himself down on a lounge in his bedroom. On the wall opposite was a bureau with a mirror. As he told Noah Brooks:

> Looking in that glass I saw myself reflected nearly at full length; but my face, I noticed had two separate and distinct images, the tip of the nose of one being about three inches from the tip of the other. I was a little bothered, perhaps startled, and got up and looked in the glass, but the illusion vanished. On lying down again, I saw it a second time, plainer, if possible, than before; and then I noticed that one of the faces was a little paler—say five shades—than the other. I got up, and the thing melted away, and I went off, and in the excitement of the hour forgot all about it—nearly, but not quite, for the thing would once in a while come up, and give me a little pang as if something uncomfortable had happened. When I went home again that night I told my wife about it, and a few days afterward I made the experiment again, when (with a laugh), sure enough! the thing came back again; but I never succeeded in bringing the ghost back after that, though I once tried very industriously to show it to

my wife, who was somewhat worried about it. She thought it was a "sign" that I was to be elected to a second term of office, and that the paleness of one of the faces was an omen that I should not see life through the last term.[1]

In response to reading the above recollection, poet Julianna Baggott, who previously had written the poem "Mary Todd on Her Deathbed" in 1999, wrote a thirty-one-line poem called "An Open Letter to Mrs. Lincoln," in just under fifteen minutes. The poem was an exercise published on the website *Quickmuse,* whose purpose is to see if first thoughts are indeed the best.[2] Here, as in her previous poem on Mary Lincoln, Baggott empathizes and sympathizes with one who became a tormented widow.

An Open Letter to Mrs. Lincoln

I see ghosts of myself
            veiled remnants of former selves
caught in whirls as if seen through moths
or bedsheets
         through the delicate clockwork of age
the paling of this life—the dust of children,
the lint of love in my pockets.
                 It's an omen
that we all know too well. Death, Mrs. Lincoln,
it's upon us.
       It lurches in the molded kitchen.
It's caught in the lame dog's funnel.
(Don't bite the sutures.)

1. Noah Brooks, *Washington in Lincoln's Time* (1895; repr. New York, Rinehart and Company, 1958), 199.
2. Published online at *Quickmuse* (http://www.quickmuse.com/), October 2008.

It's restless in the meadow of our discontent.
(There are no more meadows. There is only
discontent.) I am wearing the tall hat of my
decay—a fallen hat, so
                calicified, bent in two—
arthritic hat—oh scoliosis—how the back brace
didn't fix me then and nothing will fix me now.
For here, on display
        in the box seats, you and I sit—
Mrs. Lincoln, we were once wee pretty things that
grew squat with fever and madness and loss.
The shot will ring out. We will hear it before anyone
else because we know the chamber, the bullet.
Omen after omen after omen. We collect them
like snow globes. We shake them
                        in our fists,
watch the snow grow paler,
                paler and then paler still.

Julianna Baggott

2009

While researching, reading, and compiling an anthology of poetry about Mary Lincoln, how can one not be moved to write poetry? History does not have to be prosaic, and as both historian and poet I found myself drawn into my own musings about this woman whom Michael Meng has termed a "dark lily."

In the years I have spent researching and writing articles and books about Mary Lincoln, I always have found her to be a remarkable and fascinating woman, largely misunderstood, often wrongly maligned, and deserving of great honesty about her as well as sympathy for her. Unfortunately, I often am criticized merely for my maleness, as if my gender prevents me from understanding who Mary Lincoln was.

I see Mary in my mind "in a world that was and now is poised above time," as the Irish poet Patrick Kavanagh once wrote. She always will be there, just out of reach, bright and tremendous, blackened and vulnerable, the auroral hour to each morning of her husband's love.

Epistle for Mary Lincoln

Dear Mary, they tell me that my kindling for you
Will never brook a fire, they stare
And smirk and snort at my pile of broken starts,
My manhood just a joke upon the air,

2012

Mary Lincoln was a complex person who had numerous positive and enviable qualities and, unfortunately, many unaccountable, unenviable, and downright negative ones. She was a faithful wife, an adoring mother, and, at times, a loving friend; she tried to be an admirable first lady, and she often visited military camps and hospitals to give assistance and attention to wounded soldiers. But, as the historical record shows, Mary was also selfish, greedy, narcissistic, self-pitying, and at times downright cruel. This duality of personality perhaps was best expressed in a memoir by presidential secretary William O. Stoddard, whose main job was to deal with Mrs. Lincoln. He wrote: "It was not easy, at first, to understand why a lady who could be one day so kindly, so considerate, so generous, so thoughtful and so hopeful, could, upon another day, appear so unreasonable, so irritable, so despondent, so even niggardly, and so prone to see the dark, the wrong side of men and women and events."[1]

The historiography of Mary Lincoln is similar to her personality—some books and writers hold her up as a flawless feminist icon, while others decry her as a heartless termagant who made the lives of everyone around her insufferable. Whether fair or not, Mary's legacy has become focused on her institutionalization to a sanitarium in 1875 and whether or not she was "crazy," not just during that year, but throughout her life. As part of her insanity,

---

1. William O. Stoddard, *Inside the White House in War Times*, ed. Michael Burlingame (1890; repr. Lincoln: University of Nebraska press, 2000), 33.

history typically recounts Mary's penchant—even mania—for shopping, as well as her belief in spiritualism, or communicating with the spirits of her dead loved ones. Most writers tend to use these aspects of Mary's personality as a starting point to either defend her as an abused woman, the victim of a misogynist society (and misogynist historical community), or to declare her insanity as further proof of her reprehensible character.

No matter how these character traits are viewed, they have generally become Mary's primary fame.

It is oddly fitting, then, that the most recent poems published about Mary—and the concluding pieces in this book—deal with all three of these qualities. In his "Mary Lincoln Triptych," poet R. T. Smith said he was moved to write his trilogy of poems after reading a number of books about Mary Lincoln and finding himself captivated by her. "I discovered scores of fascinating things about Mary Todd Lincoln, but the ones that struck the most resonant chord involved her obsessive shopping, her immersion in spiritualism and her arrest on charges of insanity," Smith explained. "Beyond the numerous personal losses she experienced, I imagine Mrs. Lincoln kept a kind of national casualty count in her heart, but she tried to insulate herself from all that grief with the gloves and other purchases, while she also mourned dramatically and attempted to summon the dead, which was very much the fashion of the day. She was also far more sophisticated, erudite and sympathetic than I had guessed, and by the time I was a few pages into note taking, I was captivated and wanted to find a voice that would do her justice."[2]

The first of Smith's three poems, "Gloves," examines Mary Lincoln's dual nature of being stingy and parsimonious while simultaneously spending lavishly on her own wardrobe and on White House decorating. The poem "Summoning Shades" delves into Mary's profound personal grief due to the deaths of her husband and three of her four children; it also explores her belief in spiritualism as an anodyne to ease her suffering and broken heart. In Smith's final poem, "A Serpent's Tooth," he deals with what he believes was an "open hostility" between Mary and her oldest son Robert, the son who had her put on trial for insanity and committed to a sanitarium in

2. R. T. Smith, "Mary Lincoln Triptych," *The Missouri Review* (Winter 2012): 119–33.

1875. Specifically, Mary's voice in the poem is looking back one year later about the "torture and insult" of Bellevue Place. Smith has described his triptych as "three monologues" that he hopes "will allow a credible version of [Mary's] voice to be heard today."

Smith's "Mary Lincoln Triptych" was published in the Winter 2012 issue of *The Missouri Review*, and received the 2013 Gerald T. Perkoff Literary Prize in Poetry.

(Editor's note: the length of this triptych, combined with the number of historical allusions in the poem, made it desirable to include clarifying endnotes within the piece.)

Gloves
October 1862

> *Thrift, thrift Horatio . . . .*

Spendthrift, you say? No, but also yes.
Entre nous: Finesse is everything, and if

I cover my fingers with precious fabric—calf
leather or velvet, silk of shantung
or charmeuse—my fine hands will dance,
despite all the jet and ebony of my mourning.

Sackcloth and ashes will not bring sweet Willie back,
and since I have drained bereavement's cup
and wept myself dry, the sprigs of funeral myrtle
are now forbidden. So I must uncocoon
and hide the martyr's face from my surviving boys.
Let Victoria remain the priestess of misery[3];

3. England's Queen Victoria lost her beloved consort, Prince Albert, in December 1861 and wore widow's weeds until her death in 1901. Victoria made mourning almost fashionable, some historians have argued. In Victoria, Mary Lincoln saw a kindred spirit. After President Lincoln's assassination, Victoria wrote a letter of condolence to America's

I will display a survivor's poise,
keep Tad and Robert by my side
as I visit afflicted soldiers from the killing fields.

But every spending spree, mind you, is designed
to distract from migraines like thunderstorms
within me.[4] Less mania than calculation,
my millinery outings with retinue and etiquette
preserve me, and I have my advocates:

Poor sons too good to dwell on this unworthy earth,
Eddie and Willie both in séance somberly
entreat: *Mother do not neglect*
elegance, which amplifies both your elevated station

and grief itself. Lizzie Keckley (who knows
the White House staff call me Hellcat
for my tantrums, which are not excessive)
says this: custom gloves are the luxuries the senators'
ladies will likely eye with most envy,

ribboned gloves, those open at the wrist with pearl buttons,
dove-colored, chantilly, seamed, hush-blue, those suited

for the opera or riding, mittens for frost, every cut and cloth,
gloves . . . and fans—the Italian, the Japanese laced
with figures like fantastic shadows and spreading
wing-like with one flick of my wrist. Because Father
shares his many secrets and seeks advice,

---

first lady. Mary Lincoln replied that she was "deeply grateful for its expressions of tender
sympathy, coming as they do, from a heart which from its own sorrow, can appreciate
the *intense grief* I now endure." Queen Victoria to Mary Lincoln, Apr. 29, 1865, and Mary
Lincoln to H. M. Queen Victoria, Washington, May 21, 1865, Turner and Turner, *Mary
Todd Lincoln,* 230–31. Original letter to Mary from the queen is in Frame 43634, Abraham
Lincoln Papers, Library of Congress.
    4. Mary Lincoln suffered from severe migraines her entire life.

calls me his "Kitchen Cabinet," they hate me,
all the pullets in their leg-o-mutton sleeves
and empire waists. I am woven like a silken thread
in jacquard through this war,

and they but bystanders, jackals under their bonnet
brims, such halos of the ordinary I have to laugh.

Sometimes in the Green Room I see Willie and nearly
lose all resolve—but pinch my wrist, stiffen up.

How they would outdo me, though,
with damask floral patterns, ashes-of-rose
and parlor wit, but I am more eloquent in French,

which few can match. I will teach
them how we scorn in Illinois, and I can glare
across a *soirée* with lethal frost,
or exchange candid glances with the sovereign
of this whole nation, flutter my gloved fingers in a wave,
that Mr. Lincoln may smile amid his woes.

Grief: no more frill and fringe.
Leave the canary yellow, magenta flounce
and cobweb shawl to the hussies of the punch bowl,
harridans of the whisper and *politesse*.

Yet I sustain my smile, *noblesse oblige . . . oubliette.*

Debt, of course, hovers,
and in private, without his corvid uniform
and cannon hat, he will admonish me: *Pray, Mother,*
how can I pay Haughwout's, Galt's Emporium, Mr. Stewart,
and all the rest of your glovers while our soldiers
in the field have no blankets?

But his heart knows we are a symbol and must shine.

Silhouette and embellishment now, without the rainbow,
yet they will flatter me, say I ravish the eye
with my bell shape and grace, my reticent attire. A lie,
yet my purple iris overlay, passing
for sable, puts their rose and emerald in the shade.

Last night I overheard
Mr. Lincoln confide to Seward, *Her flub-a-dubs*
overwhelm me. Her shopping will stink in the land,[5]
but what are eighteen pair of gloves
when he commands millions
to be spent, and not for love. *Shoes and boots again,*
madam, he complains, but no bloodshed follows me,
no *fleuve sanglant,* and neither amethyst brooch
nor tiered sleeve ever set the pandemonium torch

to any city. That harpy Mercy Conkling has dubbed me
Her Royal Highness, and the screech owl Hannah
Blaine hisses *Madame Excess,* though I do love pearls
and fresh jasmine, dining on duck and terrapin—
Parisian, but all in just proportion.

How few understand the heavy hours, how deeply
I went into weeping for my boys,
but I am recovered enough to know a First Lady
must astonish the *vox populi* and bask.

---

5. Secretary of State William H. Seward. According to Lincoln's commissioner of public buildings, Benjamin Brown French, when the president learned his wife overspent her congressional appropriation to refurbish the White House, he said, "It would stink in the nostrils of the American people to have it said that the President of the United States had approved a bill overrunning an appropriation for $20,000 for *flub dubs* for this damned old house, when the soldiers cannot have blankets." Benjamin Brown French to Pamela French, Washington, D.C., Dec. 24, 1861, French Family Papers, Library of Congress.

In taffeta silks and velvet, all my fine blacks,
I'll act the basilisk.
First the slow smolder,
but a sheathed hand can flash faster than the eye
and consign the gossips to ice
or the flames of Satan.

Once again the migraine sparks beneath my
picturesque *coronet noire,* my private burden.

Willie's face swirls in a marble pattern. What solution?

Thrift? Thank you, no, not this *grande dame.*
I'll promenade, spit fire. Somehow I'll thrive.

❧

Summoning Shades
St. Catherine's Spa, Canada: June, 1873

Willie had come forth as all in our spirit circle
of clasped hands watched a candle flicker like forsythia
in wind, yet the air was still. His voice was an echo,
a soft song wafting through water.
He told us of endless bluebell meadows
and ripe cherries falling into his hands.
He said Tad was with him now among the shades, and I was
forgiven all my parties and other adult follies.

  Veiled, I sail under false flags to test every mystic,
that they will not guess my famous sons and Mr. Lincoln
are the voices I eagerly seek. Can I trust them at all,
my faculties so shaken by grief?

Last night Frau Lili Hausman seemed honest enough,
a genuine vehicle, until the sudden disruption.

Willie floated on the verge of a revelation
when we startled at a knock, not from beyond
but at the door, and in moments lantern beams flooded
the sacred chamber: our medium was seized
and arrested by royal constables for fraud and theft
of a necklace. Heaven help us.

The bereft are vulnerable as leverets in the nest.

Of course, we all admit the speculative arts are rife
with charlatans. As any wit can see: we who seek messages
from Summerfield are desperate, which does not mean
we are misguided. Listen:

  I have trembled in darkened parlors, watching the ectoplasm
rise to duplicate faces of the departed—
one doctor's jonquil of a daughter,
a weeping Quaker's husband fallen under a trolley in Boston.
Lord knows Mr. Lincoln took his skepticism
to the grave, but now he hovers above me, an angel
christened by misfortune. He often fills the vessel
of the medium and says, *Take heart.*

I sometimes wish less fortunate war widows
could pilgrim this far north to see Niagara's great weeping
and find comfort in the cataracts, which shimmer
with white mist that could be a portal to our darlings,
despite the scoffing of cynics who say a séance is theater
for simpletons. Friends and enemies alike claim
clairvoyance is no more honest than a carnival mirror.

Even dearest Robert, who mutes
his disapproval . . . but I can guess those storms behind his eyes.
Who knows his true heart?

Scripture records the intimates of Job counted his suffering just,
reasoning, as he bathed in dust, he must have sinned deeply,
but how have I deserved such wealth of loss?

If the dead have answers, why not ask?

And if our rites are merely drama, with their hush
and curtains, shadow play and suspension
of disbelief . . . why, we make Tragedy
reverse—Lear howling for his precious dove,
Hecuba mourning her many sons as she transforms to a hound—
had they faith, they would know eternal peace
and pursue its mysteries. It is not sickness. At least
Sally Orne and Myra Bradwell[6] stand by me and see
in this seeking some dignity,
which is not easy when the body heaves with sobs,
and even in the face of public ridicule
the essence yearns for release.

But last night was a low moment,
as speechless, we watched the constables twist the key
in Lili's manacles, and I wondered that the spirit guides
could not assist her, as her features
assumed a tragic mask. Before the officers left,
the necklace was seized, a wondrous circle of gems
so deep their green was nearly night. Explanations
may be forthcoming, but is there not distress
enough in our corporeal realm to satisfy any demon?
No doubt my name will soon see newsprint again.

6. Mary's two closest friends in the years after her husband's death.

Everyone asserts the history of this endeavor is twisted,
and now the Fox sisters who first heard spirit telegraphy
have confessed to deceit,[7] but others are authentic
and desire not to swindle so much as unleash the healing secrets.
    Mr. Mumler, for instance, whom I visited just this year
under the *nomme de guerre* of Mrs. Tydall,
never guessed my identity, and detected nothing unusual
through the lens, but when he lifted the silver print
from its chemical fixer, he was amazed as I
to see Mr. Lincoln clearly visible behind me, hands resting
on my shoulders in his former fashion, face placid
in death. The image was unmistakable, and I have copies yet
to overwhelm the skeptics who shall set in
like wolves to discredit Mumler's conjury as "counterfeit."[8]

Possession and loss—we all learn the sequence,
but how we suffer who could not honor the gods of proportion.

    The Lauries of Georgetown told me: "Mary, your excess
is selfish, it is time to resume living," even as they summoned Father
from the crepuscular beyond, and Nettie Colburn's
usual guide Pinkie assured me the President
was happier where no cabinet traitors
plotted against him and called him "our gorilla" in secret.[9]

7. Margaret and Kate Fox were two sisters from near Rochester, N.Y., who started the Spiritualism movement in 1848 when they claimed to be able to decode rapping noises made by spirits. In 1888, the sisters admitted their work was a hoax, that they made the noises themselves.

8. William H. Mumler was a "spirit photographer" in Boston who claimed to be able to capture the images of a person's dead loved ones in his photographs. Mary Lincoln visited his studio in 1872 under a false name. The resulting picture of Mary Lincoln dressed in her widow's weeds shows two spirits standing behind her, her son Tad over her right shoulder and her husband, President Lincoln, over her left shoulder. It is easily the most famous picture of Mary Lincoln ever taken.

9. The Lauries and Nettie Colburn were spiritualist mediums whom Mary frequently visited and consulted while she was first lady. For firsthand accounts of Mary's visits to spiritualists, see Nettie Colburn Maynard's 1917 book, *Was Abraham Lincoln a Spiritualist?*

He awaits only my arrival to complete his serenity,
as they dwell in an Elysian demesne, and their only worry
is the safety of those stranded this side of the river.

Is it not great comfort for a starved heart to feel the departed
surround you as a cloud? That is my sensation
in mid-trance. I, also, doubt
much of the rattling and automatic writing, the jingling bells,
aromas to stimulate memory, but voices of my boys
and husband are another matter. I am soothed but can never
hear enough and afterwards yearn to journey beyond the veil.

Even visitations in Europe yielded little succor,
as Mr. Lincoln appeared above a Tuscan chapel's altar,
and I followed Tad, then little Eddie through winding
Kinderstrauss in Baden-Baden, their laughter
as from the past playing tag through our own labyrinth
now occupied by that butcher Grant,
who has seemed unmoved by so much slaughter.
I always drink in the sounds of my beloved
like a desert absorbing water.

Tonight I will again in secret approach death's threshold—
the cool mists and hushes around a skirted table
where we form a human wreath
hoping the shadows will consent to speak.

If twilight must become my one safe haven on earth,
it is fitting. After all, I was born a Todd,
and *tod* in German says *death,*
which Willie promises nightly is sweeter than any sleep.

A Serpent's Tooth
Springfield, Illinois: May 1876

I held my tongue, though even in shock,
that is not my nature,
but this morning a bluebird is singing Union blue
in the orchard, his feathers the core of a gas jet's
flame. At last I can journey back
to my indictment and captivity, the suffering my one
surviving son inflicted. A year. I will not say his name.
Hell is in my heart, but madness was never my burden.

  Could croquet and hammocks, carriage rides
and endless tea, rose gardens to rival the Tuilleries tame
the truly demented? Atmosphere was everything, civility,
but Dr. Patterson's remedies were just the sort of sham
men forever devise to fetter an able woman's capacities,
and they will always style it *chivalry*.

  I confess to torturous headaches, joints aflame, palpitations,
the fitting grief of one who has lost so many.
And was Mrs. Lincoln "prone to purchase in excess,
then grow desperate concerning money?"
Yes, I tried to sell the costumes meant to make a First Lady
inspiring. I sewed bonds into my petticoats
but also endured fevers and weeping—
my muscles burning, the shakes, my running waters.
They gave me Squibb chloral hydrate in bitter solution,
which kept me close to lethargy,
and I shrieked back only in spirit when admonished.

History's widows have been prone to ailments few others
can fathom. Woe to those who must "seek asylum."
The condition, in French, is *aliénation*. Precisely.

  But set it all aside, even if I did see spies at every corner
(I now know the Pinkertons and servants lurked,
RTL's agents seeking to record every gesture.)
Did that make me Pandora?

Tomorrow marks the anniversary,
and he is once again devising petitions to return me
to that Bellevue Plantation for the Off-Kilter and Crazed
(not, of course, the name they dare display on the gate,
nor the bucolic brochures of ivied lies).

  And so they came, Mr. Leonard Swett[10] and his officers,
to lead me straight—in handcuffs—into court to answer
charges. In the Windy City the law requires any persons suspected
of unsound mind be indicted with the crime
of insanity—note: the *crime*. So long as the bluebird
spirits from tree to tree I can disclose the horrors.
No one spoke for me, my own counsel sharing
the conviction that I was *non compos mentis,*
required supervision to prevent me from self harm,
and I was supposed a danger to even loved ones. Barristers
and solicitors, evidence given by clerks and notaries,
sums and inventories—all that masculine quackery was mustered
to put me away. The Bard has an answer for lawyers.
And the doctors in their whiskers were in the main
men I had never met, though they rattled off such diagnoses!

10. One of Abraham Lincoln's closest friends, a top Chicago attorney and one of the two
men whom Robert Lincoln turned to in the years after his father's death when he needed
advice and assistance. It was Swett who went to Mary's hotel room in 1875 and brought
her to court to face charges of insanity brought against her by Robert.

For finale, my son spoke through sobs, the cost
to him of holding the sacred legacy and estate
of his beloved father intact. I was bringing disgrace
and scandal to the national memory.
"Pound foolish," he said, in his pious voice, "of unsound reason,"
"a peril to herself and others." Judas boy.
And all for the sake of silver, this *Grand Guignol*.

Hopeless, I did not ascend the stand, half afraid
they would hold my Kentucky tongue against me,
as RTL sat there, his elf ears and high collar, a local civic pillar
with his official accent bland as clabber.
And it would not have mattered an inch or an ounce,
as already the newspapers were tomahawking me *sans* mercy:
"The Demented Widow," "A Nation's Shame."

Ten minutes of deliberation
served to draw their consensus conclusion:
guilty, and sentenced to exile of undisclosed duration.
Can those silk tongues not know how seeming lunacy
may mask a divine lucidity? But why even ask?

   Outside pastoral Batavia Dr. Patterson reigned
over Bellevue Place, the tenants including:
Mrs. Wheeler who ranted at dawn and pounded the floor by night,
Mrs. Edouard who would not desert her bed,
Mrs. Mungar who stabbed herself with the matron's scissors,
Mrs. Johnson who urinated on the floors in the name of God,
Mrs. Harcourt who raved and died on the premises,
poor Minnie Judd who had to be force-fed,
so desperate was she to disappear,
and then the notorious Mrs. Lincoln, whose ungrateful son
learned at Harvard to justify his every writ and edict.
Words may "fly up to heaven," yet come from another realm.

Few see the sparks upon your breath for what they were,
Or for the lilies and violets pictured in your hair,
They call it vengeance, just a word, they do not dare
To see how lovely is the pain that marks
Your face, and drove the world about you to
The brink of nothing safe or sane or heard.
I read the lies that rain about your heart,
The smoke that smarts the intemperate brain.
I see, I see the burnished arts of all you wear,
The smear and smudge of tears that dripped
Upon your well-dressed pages, pressed
Against your smoldering breast,
Your handsome letters never written for those who care,
But only for those who'll listen.

Jason Emerson

My bed, stylish, expensively ornate,
my room private, but for the hireling spinster
Elvira Ross, ingratiating but mouse-devious,
who watched me through slats at all hours.
I rocked in my comfortable chair or wrote letters,
toured the manicured grounds and conspired with my visitors
cunning as Mrs. Surratt, who kept the nest
that sheltered Booth and all his vipers.
Does such sinister comparison convey my desperation?

It was in the garden that the bluebirds first addressed me
amid the early irises frilled like petticoats,
and what they promised was freedom,
on the condition I renounce revenge. My instructions:
simply conduct yourself as if this charade were normal,
converse with muted animation,
hands clenched in your lap or busy knitting,
and follow the regimen with smiles. In short: captivate
your captors and never speak of anguish
over who has your trunks and how that nameless martinet
conducts the business of your funds
all in the name of devotion and pity.

Restrained behavior saved me from the chemical cures
favored in that *chateau* of torture:
opium, morphia, cannabis, indica, belladonna,
ergot, conium and Bellevue's celebrated whisky-laced eggnog,
all dispensed to suspend the patients in harmonious lassitude.
J'ai parlé avec les mortes,
and they will tell you mental energy is the essential elixir
for both sides of the cosmic river,
so I feign stupor but keep my quiet lightning.

Robert. There, I have said it. Robber, covert,
my monster of mankind son. His confederates
knew that voices swirled inside my head and I feared fire
beyond proportion. They amplified my symptoms
till even dear sister Elizabeth agreed it best to cozy me
in a "secure place," safe for devotees of Duty.
Even in my loony room I had to endure a sentry,
Miss Ross of the soft voice who watched me like a hawk,
and from my bluebird's whispers, I know, no mouse at all.

Now I have this terrace, no leash, the so-called freedom
of a woman wronged, then settled with caring kin.
Even the army of my enemies agree,
despite the serpent's bite, I no longer flash the aspect
of a dangerous woman, though I know
the lay of the land, country of sanity I never left.

And still the bluebird sings to me *doucement,*
brings dispatches from beyond, and the connivers
of "justice" have never guessed I have a pistol,
my one white trunk stored at the station and ready
for escape—a hooded cloak, emeralds, gowns, the Todd silver.
Ah, *mon petit oiseau bleu* flashing in the sky,
will they surprise me again? "Restored to reason"—
that lets them all sleep easily. And remorse? *Not guilty.*

Midday now, birdsong, and in the distance smoke twirls
the hue of a fawn in winter, color its only
defense. Folded in my green *rouche* sleeve I keep my final
retribution–the will, witnessed and signed lovingly,
Your dearest Mother. Let him finally comprehend and suffer
the sting: I will leave him all.

R. T. Smith

Afterword

What less useful thing could one find in the wild Kentucky of 1818 than a book of poems? Yet Mary Todd, through her family, through her tutors in French and in deportment, made use of this art, and carried the tunes with her, both physically and mentally, for sixty years. She was, in person, a leading vector of Ancient, Romantic, and Victorian culture in the cleared woods, around the slave market, to the plain prairie, and on to Washington, D.C. The present book lends a hint of that taste and a conspectus of what her life has spawned in others.

Among all the poets, perhaps she loved Byron best. That fabled, immoral lord came to be idealized by many, including the young Mary Todd and the mature Mary Lincoln, and not least because his was the poetic taste she most shared with Abraham. Yet while the husband leaned toward the rougher and bawdier rhymesters—Burns, Shakespeare, folk jesters like Artemus Ward—the well-bred wife's tastes were more refined, and it seems that heroic women of poesy were among her warmest friends. She gave gifts of a Maria Edgeworth tale to a little neighbor girl; to that girl's mother, *Early Friendships: A Tale,* by the forgotten Mrs. Copley.

Upon the quatrain of Mrs. Lincoln's four sons did she try most to inscribe the feeling for literature. They by nature enjoyed the male writers, and thus the family read aloud from the verse and adventures of Sir Walter Scott, inter alia, at home in Springfield; as late as 1864, Mary purchased some Scott to share with youngest son Tad. But her quatrain crumbled very early. One couplet came apart at Eddie's death in 1850, leaving Robert without a contemporary brother. The other couplet, so famous in their first year at the Executive Mansion, also broke, at Willie's death, leaving Tad to consort with pet animals and to struggle with books. Robert bought four volumes of Edgar Allan Poe while at Harvard; his mother seems not to have cared for such lugubriosity, at least in print. And Abraham, the principal canto of Mary's life, was also broken midway through the song.

So in the Greek tragedy of her widowhood, Mary built herself a walled garden of books, many of them poetry. Longfellow she bought like a malarial affliction, three different editions in one month before her committal in 1875; and at least one other edition, given as a gift to a minister's daughter in 1873. Perhaps she bought new copies of things she had given away . . . as she could not refill the lost paradise of sons and husbands given to death. Robert returned to sellers a few of his mother's brick wall of books, just as she had tried to return a Midas's table-worth of jewels and clothes in 1866–67; best not let the garden wall grow too tall with new bricks.

Why do we not think that manic buying of books is as redolent of disease as the dozens of footstools she owned at her death? Could poems prop up her aching soul? Or is love of Whittier, Tennyson, Josiah Holland, not the impassable sin that shopping for other stuff has come to be? For this reason: Though we have many fewer examples of Mary's allusion to poems in her letters than in Abraham's—rare was his gift for memorization and recall—we still believe that she was a vector of culture. Poets inspired her, and she continues to inspire poets, as this entirely innovative book reveals.

JAMES M. CORNELIUS
Curator, Lincoln Collection
Abraham Lincoln Presidential Library and Museum
Springfield, Illinois
St. George's Day, 2012

Bibliography

ARCHIVES

Abraham Lincoln Library and Museum, Harrogate, Tenn.
Abraham Lincoln Presidential Library, Springfield, Ill.
    Robert Todd Lincoln Family Papers
    Robert Todd Lincoln Letterpress Books
Hildene, The Lincoln Family Home, Manchester, Vt.
Illinois State Archives
Library of Congress
    French Family Papers
    John G. Nicolay Papers
    Washington During the Civil War: The Diary of Horatio Nelson Taft, 1861–1865,
        3 vols., John R. Sellers, ed.
Mary Todd Lincoln Home, Lexington, Ky.
University of Chicago Library, Department of Special Collections
    Lincoln Miscellaneous Manuscripts

NEWSPAPERS

Boston Daily Advertiser
Boston Evening Transcript
Chicago Post and Mail
Chicago Tribune
Cincinnati Daily Press

Frank Leslie's Illustrated Newspaper
Illinois Daily Journal
Jackson [Miss.] *Daily News*
Mt. Pleasant [Iowa] *News*
New York Times
Sandusky [Ohio] *Register*
Sangamo Journal
Springfield [Mass.] *Republican*
Washington *Evening Star*
Washington *National Republican*

BOOKS AND ARTICLES

Baggott, Julianna. *Lizzie Borden in Love: Poems in Women's Voices.* The Crab Or-
chard Series in Poetry. Carbondale: Southern Illinois University Press, 2006.

Baker, Jean H. *Mary Todd Lincoln: A Biography.* New York: W. W. Norton & Co., 1987.

Basler, Roy P. "The Authorship of the 'Rebecca' Letters." *Abraham Lincoln Quarterly*
2, no. 2 (June 1942): 80–90.

———, ed. *Collected Works of Abraham Lincoln.* 8 vols. New Brunswick: Rutgers
University Press, 1953.

Bayne, Julia Taft. *Tad Lincoln's Father.* 1931; repr., Lincoln and London: University
of Nebraska Press, 2001.

Betts, William W., ed. *Lincoln and the Poets.* Pittsburgh: University of Pittsburgh
Press, 1965.

Bradley, Edward Sculley. *George Henry Boker: Poet and Patriot.* Philadelphia:
University of Pennsylvania Press, 1927.

Brooks, Noah. *Washington in Lincoln's Time.* 1895; repr. New York: Rinehart and
Company, 1958.

Brussel, James A. "Mary Todd Lincoln: A Psychiatric Study." *Psychiatric Quarterly*
15, supp. 1 (January 1941): 16.

Bryant, William Cullen, ed. *The Family Library of Poetry and Song.* New York:
Fords, Howard, and Hulbert, 1870.

Burke, Margaret Sullivan. "The Home of Mrs. Mary A. Denison." *The Writer* 7,
no. 1 (Jan. 1894): 3–4.

Burlingame, Michael. "The Lincolns' Marriage: 'A Fountain of Misery, of a Quality
Absolutely Infernal,'" in *The Inner World of Abraham Lincoln* (Urbana: University
of Illinois Press, 1994), 268–355.

———. "Mary Todd Lincoln's Unethical Conduct as First Lady" in *At Lincoln's Side: John Hay's Civil War Correspondence and Selected Writings* (Carbondale: Southern Illinois University Press, 2000), 185–203.

Busey, Samuel C. *Personal Reminiscences and Recollections of Forty-Six Years' Membership in the Medical Society of the District of Columbia, and Residence in This City.* Philadelphia: Dornan, Printer, 1895.

Carmichael, Sarah E. *Poems.* Utah, 1866.

C. E. L. "A Kindly Word for Abraham Lincoln's Widow." *The Christian Register* 101, no. 36 (September 7, 1872): 1.

Del Vecchio, Thomas, ed. *Contemporary American Male Poets: An Anthology of Verse by 459 Living Poets.* New York: Henry Harrison, 1937.

Emerson, Jason. *Giant in the Shadows: The Life of Robert T. Lincoln.* Carbondale: Southern Illinois University Press, 2012.

———. *The Madness of Mary Lincoln.* Carbondale: Southern Illinois University Press, 2007.

———. "'Of Such Is the Kingdom of Heaven': The Mystery of Little Eddie." *Journal of the Illinois State Historical Society* 92, no. 3 (Autumn 1999): 201–21.

———. "The Poetic Lincoln." *Lincoln Herald* 101, no. 1 (Spring 1999): 4–12.

Emerson, Ralph Waldo. "The Poet," in Emerson, *Essays* (Boston: Houghton, Mifflin and Company, 1890), 15.

Flenniken, Kathleen. *Famous.* Lincoln: University of Nebraska Press, 2006.

Fuller, Frank. *A Day with the Lincoln Family.* New York: Hotel Irving, 1905.

Grimsley, Elizabeth Todd. "Six Months in the White House." *Journal of the Illinois State Historical Society* 19 (Oct.–Jan., 1926–27): 68–69.

Guillory, Dan. *The Lincoln Poems.* Mahomet, Ill.: Mayhaven Publishing, 2008.

Hay, Logan. "Lincoln in 1841 and 1842." *Abraham Lincoln Quarterly* 2, no. 3 (Sept. 1942): 114–26.

Heaney, Seamus. *The Redress of Poetry.* New York: Farrar, Straus and Giroux, 1995.

Helm, Katherine. *True Story of Mary, Wife of Lincoln.* New York: Harper & Brothers, 1928.

Herndon, William H., and Jesse W. Weik. *Herndon's Lincoln: The True Story of a Great Life.* Douglas L. Wilson and Rodney O. Davis, eds. 1889; repr. Urbana: University of Illinois Press, 2006.

Hertz, Emanuel. *The Hidden Lincoln: From the Letters and Papers of William H. Herndon.* New York: Viking Press, 1938.

Hickey, James T. "Robert Todd Lincoln and the 'Purely Private' Letters of the Lincoln Family," in *The Collected Writings of James T. Hickey* (Springfield: Illinois State Historical Society, 1990), 159–79.

Horton, George Moses. *Naked Genius*. Raleigh, N.C.: Wm. B. Smith & Co., 1865.

Howe, Susan, and Sheree Maxwell Bench, eds. *Discoveries: Two Centuries of Poems by Mormon Women*. Salt Lake City: Brigham Young University, 2004.

Ireland, Mary E. "Mary A. Denison." *Magazine of Poetry* 7, no. 2 (Feb. 1895): 108.

Kaplan, Fred. *Lincoln: The Biography of a Writer*. New York: HarperCollins, 2008.

Keckley, Elizabeth. *Behind the Scenes Or, Thirty Years a Slave and Four Years in the White House*. New York: G. W. Carleton, 1868.

Kinnaird, Virginia. "Mrs. Lincoln as a White House Hostess." *Papers in Illinois History and Transactions for the Year 1938* (Springfield: Illinois State Historical Society, 1939), 65–87.

Laighton, Albert. *Poems*. Boston: Brown, Taggard, and Chase, 1859.

Lincoln, Abraham. *The Poems of Abraham Lincoln*. Little Books of Wisdom Series. Bedford, Mass.: Applewood Books, 1991.

Masters, Edgar Lee. *Spoon River Anthology*. 1915; repr. New York: Macmillan Company, 1921.

McCreary, Donna. *Fashionable First Lady: The Victorian Wardrobe of Mary Lincoln*. Carmel, Ind.: Lincoln Presentations, 2007.

McMurtry, R. Gerald. "Abraham Lincoln: Poet." *Lincoln Lore* 529 (May 29, 1939).

——. "Lincoln: Poet or Rhymester?" *Lincoln Lore* 1484 (Oct. 1961).

Menz, Katherine B. *Lincoln Home Historic Furnishings Report*. Harper's Ferry, W.V.: National Park Service, 1984.

Miles, Mary Leighton. "'The Fatal First of January, 1841.'" *Journal of the Illinois State Historical Society* 20, no. 1 (April 1927): 13–48.

Miller, Della Crowder. *Abraham Lincoln: A Biographic Treatment in Sonnet Sequence*. 3 vols. Boston: Christopher Publishing House, 1965.

Miller, Marion Mills. "The Poetic Spirit of Lincoln," in Osborn H. Oldroyd, ed., *The Poets' Lincoln* (Washington, D.C., 1915).

Miller, Richard Lawrence. "Lincoln's 'Suicide' Poem: Has It Been Found?" *For the People: A Newsletter of the Abraham Lincoln Association*, 6:1 (Spring 2004): 1, 6.

Murphy, Miriam B. "Sarah Elizabeth Carmichael: Poetic Genius of Pioneer Utah." *Utah Historical Quarterly* 43, no. 1 (Winter 1975): 52–66.

N. A. "Little Eddie." *Illinois Daily Journal*, Feb. 7, 1850.

Neely, Mark E., and R. Gerald McMurty. *The Insanity File: The Case of Mary Todd Lincoln*. Carbondale: Southern Illinois University Press, 1986.

Oldroyd, Osborn H., ed. *The Poets' Lincoln; Tributes in Verse to the Martyred President*. Washington, D.C.: The Editor (Osborn H. Oldroyd), 1915.

Perkins, Reed Miles. *Prairie Poems*. Springfield, Ill.: Frye Printing, 1946.

Perry, James Raymond. "The Poetry of Lincoln." *North American Review* (Feb. 1911): 213.

Plotts, J. N., ed. *Poetical Tributes to the Memory of Abraham Lincoln.* Philadelphia: J. B. Lippincott & Co., 1865.

Poore, Ben: Perley. *Reminiscences of Sixty Years in the National Metropolis.* 2 vols. Philadelphia: Hubbard Brothers Publishers, 1886.

Pratt, Harry. "Little Eddie Lincoln—We Miss Him Very Much." *Journal of the Illinois State Historical Society* 47, no. 3 (Autumn 1954): 300–305.

———. *Personal Finances of Abraham Lincoln.* Springfield, Ill.: Abraham Lincoln Association, 1943.

Randall, Ruth Painter. *I, Mary: A Biography of the Girl Who Married Abraham Lincoln.* Boston: Little, Brown & Co., 1959.

———. *Mary Lincoln: Biography of a Marriage.* Boston: Little, Brown and Company, 1953.

Ricketts, Sarah. *A Window on Eternity: The Life and Poetry of Jane Hess Merchant.* Nashville: Abingdon Press, 1989.

Roberts, Octavia. *Lincoln in Illinois.* Boston: Houghton Mifflin, 1918.

Sandburg, Carl. *The Lincoln Collector: The Story of the Oliver R. Barrett Lincoln Collection.* New York: Bonanza Books, 1960.

Schwartz, Barry. "Ann Rutledge in American Memory: Social Change and the Erosion of a Romantic Drama." *Journal of the Abraham Lincoln Association* 26, no. 1 (Winter 2005): 1–27.

Sellers, John R., ed. *Washington During the Civil War: The Diary of Horatio Nelson Taft, 1861–1865,* 3 vols. Manuscript Division, Library of Congress. Published online, Feb. 12, 2002, www.memory.loc.gov/ammem/tafthtml/tafthome.html.

Sherman, Joan R. *The Black Bard of North Carolina: George Moses Horton and His Poetry.* Chapel Hill: University of North Carolina Press, 1997.

Steell, Willis. "Mrs. Abraham Lincoln and Her Friends." *Munsey's Magazine* 40, no. 5 (Feb. 1909): 617–23.

Stoddard, William O. *Inside the White House in War Times.* Edited by Michael Burlingame. 1890; repr. Lincoln: University of Nebraska Press, 2000.

Stoltz, Charles. *The Tragic Career of Mary Todd Lincoln.* South Bend, Ind.: Round Table, 1931.

"A Story of the Early Days in Springfield—And a Poem." *Journal of the Illinois State Historical Society* 16, nos. 1–2 (April–July 1923): 141–46.

Sutton, Amy Louise. "Lincoln and Son Borrow Books." *Illinois Libraries* 48, no. 6 (June 1966): 443–44.

Swisshelm, Jane Grey. "Tribute to the Dead." *Chicago Tribune,* July 20, 1882, 7.

Thomas, Dylan. "Poetic Manifesto," in Thomas, *Early Prose Writings,* Walford Davies, ed. (London: J. M. Dent & Sons, 1971).

Townsend, William H. *Lincoln and His Wife's Home Town.* Indianapolis: Bobbs-Merrill, 1929.

Turner, Justin, and Linda Levitt. *Mary Todd Lincoln: Her Life and Letters.* New York: Alfred A. Knopf, 1972.

Walsh, John Evangelist. *The Shadows Rise: Abraham Lincoln and the Ann Rutledge Legend.* Urbana: University of Illinois Press, 1993.

Weeks, Stephen B. "George Moses Horton: Slave Poet." *The Southern Workman* 43, no. 10 (October 1914): 571–77.

Wentworth, May, ed. *Poetry of the Pacific: Selections and Original Poems from the Poets of the Pacific States.* Pacific Publishing Company, 1867.

Wheeler, Samuel P. "Solving a Lincoln Literary Mystery: 'Little Eddie.'" *Journal of the Abraham Lincoln Association* 33, no. 2 (Summer 2012): 34–46.

Who's Who in Iowa: A Biographical Record of Iowa's Leaders in Business, Professional and Public Life. Iowa Press Association, 1940.

Williams, A. Dallas, comp. *The Praise of Lincoln: An Anthology.* Indianapolis: Bobbs-Merrill Company, 1911.

Willis, N. P. "The President's Son." *Littell's Living Age* 933 (April 19, 1862): 154.

Wilson, Douglas L. "Abraham Lincoln and 'That Fatal First of January.'" *Civil War History,* 38, no. 2 (June 1992): 101–30.

Wilson, Douglas L., and Rodney O. Davis, eds. *Herndon's Informants: Letters, Interviews, and Statements about Abraham Lincoln.* Urbana: University of Illinois Press, 1998.

Wright-Davis, Mary, comp. *The Book of Lincoln.* New York: George H. Doran, 1919.

Contributors

DR. E. H. MERRIMAN was a practicing physician in Springfield, Illinois, from 1830 to about 1851. He was a member of the upper class of the town, along with Abraham Lincoln, for whom he agreed to serve as a second when Lincoln was challenged to a duel in September 1842. Merriman left Springfield in 1851, and died in Costa Rica in 1855.

GEORGE H. BOKER was one of the leading poets and playwrights of his day, and published multiple works in each genre. *Francesca da Rimini* (1853) is the play he is best remembered for, while during the Civil War he published the volume of verse titled, *Poems of the War* (1864). Boker, once a Democrat, became a staunch supporter of President Lincoln and the Union throughout the war. He later served his country as a diplomat, first as minister to Turkey and then as minister to Russia.

MARY ANDREWS DENISON was a prolific nineteenth-century writer. She wrote more than eighty novels throughout her life, and contributed stories, poems, and juvenilia to numerous popular periodicals, including *Frank Leslie's Monthly, Harper's Weekly,* the *People's Home Journal,* and *Youth's Companion.*

GEORGE MOSES HORTON was a slave for sixty-eight years, from his birth in about 1797 until the close of the Civil War. Horton's poetry collections include *The Hope of Liberty* (1829), *Poetical Works* (1845), and *Naked Genius* (1865). He died at age eighty-six.

SARAH E. CARMICHAEL was a Mormon living in Salt Lake City, but her objection to polygamy and her marriage to an army doctor of non-Mormon background alienated her from the local community. Her only book of work, *Poems,* was published in 1866 by a group of her friends and admirers. That same year she married army surgeon Jonathan M. Williamson, who had been stationed at Camp Douglas. Shortly after her marriage, Carmichael suffered a mental breakdown of unknown origin and stopped writing poetry. She was widowed in 1882, and spent her last years in a mental hospital. She died in 1901.

MARION MILLS MILLER was a scholar of classical literature at Princeton University and wrote poetry and fiction, but was best known for his work in translation and history. He compiled, edited, or translated numerous multivolume works on Greek and Latin literature and American history throughout his life. He edited a nine-volume "centenary" edition of *The Life and Works of Abraham Lincoln* in 1907; *The Wisdom of Lincoln* and *Life of Lincoln* by Henry Clay Whitney in 1908; and aided Osborn H. Oldroyd with the latter's collection of poetic tributes to the sixteenth president, *The Poets' Lincoln,* in 1915.

MARTHA THOMAS DYALL was a schoolteacher before her marriage in 1896, and afterward a homemaker and author. She loved to write both history and poetry; contributed numerous historical sketches to *The Palimpsest,* the journal of the Iowa State Historical Society; and published poems in journals and magazines, and ultimately in a book titled, *My House and Other Poems.* She died in 1942 at age seventy-four.

COURTENAY FRASER FITE was a schoolteacher in Mississippi. She was a member of her local Vicksburg Poetry Society and was interested in local history. She died in 1962 at age 85.

REED MILES PERKINS was a Springfield, Illinois, merchant at the turn of the twentieth century. He published three books of poetry: *Prairie Poems* (1946), *The Long Trail* (1958), and *Descriptive Sonnets* (1958).

JANE MERCHANT was a prolific author of more than 3,000 poems, over 2,000 letters, dozens of prose pieces, and ten collections of her poetry. Her book of poetry *The Greatest of These* received the Best Book of Poetry award from the National League of American Pen Women, and she was awarded the Beaudoin Gemstone Award for Poetry in 1965. She died in 1972.

DELLA CROWDER MILLER published numerous books as both poet and playwright. She won the 1966 Barondess/Lincoln Award from the Civil War Round Table of New York for her verse biography *Abraham Lincoln.*

EDWARD C. LYNSKEY is a crime writer, critic, and poet living with his family near Washington, D.C. His three mysteries with private investigator Frank Johnson are *The Dirt-Brown Derby* (2006), *The Blue Cheer* (2007), and *Pelham Fell Here* (2008). His creative work has been reviewed in numerous publications such as *Publishers Weekly, Booklist,* and *Library Journal.* His work has been anthologized by St. Martin's Press, the University of Virginia Press, and Storyline Press.

JULIANNA BAGGOTT is a bestselling author of poetry, novels, and young adult books. She has published three collections of poetry and been published in the best literary publications in the country, including *Poetry, The American Poetry Review,* and *Best American Poetry.* Her work has appeared in over a hundred publications, including the *New York Times,* the *Boston Globe, Glamour, Ms., Real Simple,* and read on NPR's *Here and Now* and *Talk of the Nation.* Her website is www.juliannabaggott.com.

LAURENCE OVERMIRE is popularly known as "The Genealogist-Poet," and has had a multifaceted career as writer, actor, director and educator. His award-winning poetry has been widely published in the United States and abroad in hundreds of magazines, journals, and anthologies. His plays include *Slingshot, A Woman in Washington's Army,* and *A Scrooge Mart Christmas Carol.* He served as executive producer of the Writer's Lab, a non-profit organization in Hollywood to promote quality writing in the entertainment industry, and has been involved in teaching in the arts for over 25 years. His website is www.laurenceovermire.com.

KATHLEEN FLENNIKEN'S poems have appeared in numerous journals such as *Poetry, The Iowa Review, The Southern Review,* and *Prairie Schooner.* Her first collection, *Famous,* winner of the 2005 Prairie Schooner Prize, was named a 2007 Notable Book of the Year by the American Library Association (ALA) and a finalist for the Washington State Book Award. She is a coeditor and president of Floating Bridge Press, an all-volunteer non-profit press dedicated to publishing Washington State poets. Her website is www.kathleenflenniken.com.

DAN GUILLORY is professor emeritus of English at Milliken University and the author of the poetry volumes *House Poems* (Mayhaven Publishing, 2013) *The Lincoln Poems* (Mayhaven Publishing, 2008) and *The Alligator Inventions* (Stormline Press, 1992). He has won awards or grants from the Academy of American Poets, the American Library Association, the Illinois Arts Council, and the National Endowment for the Humanities. He has served as poet in the schools for the Illinois Arts Council and as a road scholar for the Illinois Humanities Council.

MICHAEL MENG is a retired elementary school teacher from southern California, with a master's degree in American history. He currently devotes himself to writing historical poetry and prose. Meng's unpublished volume of poetry, *Abraham Lincoln: From the Wilderness to the White House*, was displayed at the Abraham Lincoln Presidential Library and Museum in 2009. He recently completed an anthology of poems on the life of Mary Lincoln titled, *The Dark Lily: A Commemorative Poetry for the Life and Times of Mary Todd Lincoln*.

JASON EMERSON is a historian, poet, and journalist from upstate New York. He has written or edited five books about members of the Lincoln family, including three on Mary Lincoln's insanity case and a biography of Robert T. Lincoln. His most recent book is *Mary Lincoln's Insanity Case: A Documentary History* (University of Illinois Press, 2013). His poems have appeared in journals such as *The Powhatan Review, Red River Review, The Rectangle, Mobius, Caveat Lector,* and *The Comstock Review.* His website is www.jasonemerson.com.

R.T. SMITH is writer-in-residence at Washington and Lee University, where he edits the literary journal *Shenandoah.* He is the author of dozens of collections of poems, most recently *In the Night Orchard: Selected Poems* (2014), and four collections of stories. His work has been reprinted in the Best American Anthologies of fiction, poetry, and mystery stories. He has received the Carole Weinstein Poetry Prize given by the Library of Virginia for Achievement in Poetry and in fall 2015 was the distinguished professor of poetry at Appalachian State University.

www.ingramcontent.com/pod-product-compliance
Lightning Source LLC
Chambersburg PA
CBHW021405090426
42742CB00009B/1009